Feedback for Learning

Teachers may be surrounded by feedback and involved in it every day, but the notion is poorly analysed and poorly used. This book provides an important collection of contributions to the highly topical theme of feedback to support learning.

The book spans three major areas which affect all teachers:

- young people's learning
- teachers' learning
- organisational learning

The authors critically examine the assumption that feedback necessarily has positive learning outcomes and describe models and practices which are more likely to result in effective learning at the individual, group and organisational level.

Feedback for Learning is important reading for teachers, heads and other senior managers in schools, as well as for all involved in giving feedback to schools.

Susan Askew is a lecturer and member of the group *Assessment, Guidance and Effective Learning* at the Institute of Education, University of London. All the contributions are written by current and past members of the group.

Feedback for Learning

Edited by Susan Askew

Written by members of the group
*Assessment, Guidance and Effective
Learning* at the Institute of Education,
University of London

London and New York

First published 2000
by RoutledgeFalmer
11 New Fetter Lane, London EC4P 4EE

Simultaneously published in the USA and Canada
by Routledge
29 West 35th Street, New York, NY 10001

RoutledgeFalmer is an imprint of the Taylor & Francis Group

Selection and editorial matter © 2000 Susan Askew; © 2000
individual chapters, their contributors.

Typeset in Sabon by M Rules
Printed and bound in Great Britain by
Biddles Ltd, Guildford and King's Lynn

British Library Cataloguing in Publication Data
A catalogue record for this book is available from the British
Library

Library of Congress Cataloging in Publication Data
Feedback for learning/edited by Susan Askew.
    p. cm.
    Includes bibliographical references and index.
    1. Learning. 2. Feedback (Psychology). 3. Interaction
analysis in education. I. Askew, Susan.
    LB1060.F44 2000
    370.15′23–dc21   00-034480

ISBN 0-415-23771–8(hbk)
ISBN 0-415-23772–6(pbk)

Contents

Figures and tables

Contributors

Susan Askew has taught in secondary schools and in higher education for twenty-five years. She is the course leader for the MA in Health Education and Health Promotion at the Institute of Education. Her research interests include collaboration for effective learning, home-school relationships, raising self-esteem and boys' behaviour and achievement. She has recently written, with Eileen Carnell, *Transforming Learning: individual and global change* (Cassell 1998).

Eileen Carnell is a senior lecturer in Personal and Social Education. Her recent research area is concerned with Teachers' Professional Development. Recent publications include 'Developing learning-centred professional practice', *Professional Development Today* (forthcoming 2000) and *Transforming Learning: individual and global change* (Cassell 1998) with Susan Askew. She is working on a new book *Supporting Young People's Learning in Secondary Schools* with Caroline Lodge (forthcoming 2001). Before joining the Institute of Education Eileen was an Inspector for Staff Development and Personal, Social and Health Education, Director of an Inner London Teachers' Centre, and action research project team member.

Shirley Clarke was a primary teacher, a maths adviser and co-ordinator of the CATs Key Stage One Test Development Agency before becoming a member of AGEL at the Institute of Education. Her work involves national and international INSET and research on formative assessment. Her publications include the *Tracking Significant Achievement* series and the best-selling *Targeting Assessment in the Primary Classroom*.

Karen Elliot is a research officer. She is involved in various projects, such as the Raising School Standards Value Added project, the

Effective Provision of Pre-school Education project and the National Evaluation of New Community Schools in Scotland. Her areas of interest include value added measures, pupil performance data and the feedback of data to schools. Previously, Karen taught languages in secondary schools in England, France and Switzerland.

Caroline Gipps is Deputy Vice Chancellor at Kingston University, having been Professor of Education at the University of London Institute of Education. Previously a primary school teacher and a career researcher, she has studied early national assessment programmes (the Assessment of Performance Unit); standardised testing in schools, programmes for allocating pupils to special needs provision, the introduction of National Curriculum assessment in primary schools; gender and other equal opportunity issues in assessment; and teacher feedback to young children. Caroline has published widely on policy and practice in assessment, and was President of the British Educational Research Association (BERA). Her book *A Fair Test? Assessment, Achievement and Equity*, written jointly with Patricia Murphy, won the SCSE prize for the best Education book published in 1994.

Eleanore Hargreaves has recently finished working on an ESRC-funded project investigating teaching, assessment and feedback strategies used by primary school teachers. Currently, she is researching on a DFID-funded international project about multigrade teaching and she also teaches on the Masters Degree in Evaluation and Assessment. Previously, Eleanore worked as Senior Research Officer for the National Foundation for Educational Research, where she developed and evaluated National Assessments for seven year olds in England and Wales. She has also spent five years teaching and researching in Egypt.

Caroline Lodge served in urban comprehensive schools for a quarter of a century in Coventry and London as class teacher, head of department, head of year, deputy head and headteacher. Her research interests are learning and school improvement, and she works as a tutor on the MA in School Effectiveness and School Improvement and as a freelance consultant, trainer and writer.

Jacqui MacDonald is a lecturer in Careers Education and Guidance (CEG), and course tutor for the Advanced Diploma in CEG and staff development facilitator for academic staff. She has wide experience of co-ordinating careers work in schools, colleges and higher education. Her areas of interest include action planning, work-related activities, vocational education and careers training for teachers. Jacqui's publications have included chapters on equal opportunities, action planning, careers resource centres and careers and the whole curriculum. Her most recent work includes a DfEE publication *Careers Education and Guidance: what every teacher needs to know* (1998). She is just about to publish a study on black professionals in the UK, *Composing Success: interviews with Black professionals*. She is a member of several professional bodies including NACGT, NICEC, BBC Secondary Education Committee and the PYBT.

Bet McCallum was a primary headteacher and INSET provider before joining the Institute of Education as course tutor to the Advanced Diploma in Education (Curriculum Studies and the Primary School), and as senior researcher on two major ESRC-funded projects (National Assessment in Primary Schools, Key Stage 1 and Key Stage 2). Her work has also included commissioned studies from NUT, SCAA, ISEIC and the CTC Trust. She has published many articles which relate to assessment in primary schools and co-authored with Caroline Gipps and others *Intuition or Evidence? Teachers and National Assessment of Seven Year Olds* (Open University Press 1995). She has a particular interest in teachers' intuitive judgements.

Jane Reed is Coordinating Director with Pam Sammons of ISEIC, the International School Effectiveness and Improvement Centre, and a freelance Education Consultant, having previously been a senior LEA adviser for Evaluation and Assessment and Director of an LEA Professional Development Centre. She works on school improvement projects in a number of schools and LEAs. She is author with Barbara MacGilchrist and Kate Myers of *The Intelligent School*. She co-ordinates ISEIC's work with LEAs and schools and is also the Director of a small charitable trust that promotes ecological citizenship.

Pam Sammons is Professor of Education and Coordinating Director of ISEIC, with Jane Reed. She has directed a number of major school effectiveness studies involving both primary and secondary schools during the past twenty years. She is author of *Forging Links: effective schools and effective departments* (Paul Chapman 1997) and *School Effectiveness: coming of age in the 21st century* (Swets & Zeitlinger 1999). Her publications also include *School Matters* (Paul Chapman 1994) with Peter Mortimore and Louise Stoll, and *Key*

Characteristics of Effective Schools (OFSTED/Institute of Education 1995). She is currently involved in the first major study in the UK to focus specifically on the effectiveness of early years education, Effective Provision of Pre-School Education, and is co-directing the national evaluation of New Community Schools in Scotland.

Rebecca Smees is a research officer. Her background is in psychology and statistics and she has worked at the Institute of Education since 1994. She has been involved in Value Added projects at the primary and secondary level such as projects for Lancashire LEA, Jersey LEA and Surrey LEA. She is also involved in research into pupils' attitudes in Lancashire and Scotland (the Improving School Effectiveness Project).

Louise Stoll is Professor of Education and Head of the Professional Learning and Development Group at the University of Bath. Formerly, she was Co-ordinating Director of ISEIC, where she established the School Improvement Network, having previously been a primary teacher, researcher on *School Matters* and co-director for the Halton Effective Schools Project in Canada. She is involved in teaching, accredited training and development work with schools in all phases and LEAs. Her research includes Improving School Effectiveness for the SOEID and Effective School Improvement for the EU. She is co-author of *School Matters* (Paul Chapman 1984) and *Changing Our Schools* (Open University Press 1996) and *No Quick Fixes* (Falmer Press 1998). Forthcoming publications include *Learning* (with Dean Fink and Lorna Earl, RoutledgeFalmer).

Brenda Taggart is a research officer currently working on the Effective Provision of Pre-school Education Project, having worked on a number of research projects, most recently in the field of primary assessment. Brenda has worked in primary schools as a teacher, deputy head and acting head. She was an Advisory Teacher for Primary Education for the ILEA and has worked extensively in the field of INSET, having run an LEA Teachers' Centre. She has been a tutor on the Primary Post-Graduate Certificate in Education (PGCE) course at the Institute.

Sally Thomas trained as a psychologist and over the last seventeen years has worked at both Oxford University and the London School of Economics. She is currently a senior research lecturer at the Institute of Education and directs several projects including the Lancashire Value Added project set up in 1992. Her research interests include school evaluation, effectiveness and improvement, assessment, multilevel modelling and international comparisons. She has acted as a consultant to various international projects and has received funding from ESRC, European Union, OFSTED, DFEE and DENI among others.

Chris Watkins is a senior lecturer and head of the academic group *Assessment, Guidance and Effective Learning*. Having been a teacher and school counsellor, his areas of work include mentoring, tutoring, effective learning in classrooms and school behaviour. He is course tutor to the MA in Effective Learning and the MA in School Development, and a member of the team currently completing an ESRC project 'The Violence-resilient School'. Recent publications include *Effective Learning*, with Eileen Carnell, Caroline Lodge and others (1996); *Learning about Learning* with Eileen Carnell, Caroline Lodge and others (National Association for Pastoral Care in Education 1998; RoutledgeFalmer 2000); *Managing Classroom Behaviour* (Association for Teachers and Lecturers 1998; Institute of Education 1999; Scottish Consultative Council on the Curriculum 2000), *Improving School Behaviour* with P. Wagner (Paul Chapman/Sage 2000); *Tomorrow's Schools: towards integrity* with Caroline Lodge and R. Best (eds) (RoutledgeFalmer 2000). Chris has been an executive member of the National Association for Pastoral Care in Education since 1982.

Felicity Wikeley took up a senior lectureship at the University of Bath in May 2000. Previously she was a senior lecturer and an Associate Director of the International School Effectiveness and Improvement Centre. She was also course leader for the School Effectiveness and School Improvement MA and EdD specialist pathway. She has researched and worked with schools on a variety of school effectiveness and school improvement issues including personal learning planning, pupil approaches to subject option choice and teacher appraisal. Her other research interests include school communities and the relationship between parents and their children's schools.

1 Gifts, ping-pong and loops – linking feedback and learning

Susan Askew and Caroline Lodge

It may seem that feedback is a rather small notion to write a whole book about. However, we suggest that it is time that understandings about feedback in education are examined more closely. In this chapter we adopt a broad definition of feedback which includes all dialogue to support learning in both formal and informal situations. We argue that this dialogue will be influenced by different views of learning and we need to explore feedback alongside associated beliefs about learning, to consider how feedback can be most effective in promoting learning.

Learning is increasingly being recognised as complex. Many writers now recognise the importance of the emotional and social dimension of learning as well as the cognitive (Askew and Carnell 1998; Epstein 1993; Goleman 1996; International Commission on Education for the Twenty-first Century 1996; Whitaker 1995). The relationship between learning and teaching is being viewed as a dynamic process, rather than a one-way transmission of knowledge (Askew and Carnell 1998; Biggs and Moore 1993; Watkins *et al.* 1996). Learning is supported by a whole range of processes, one of which is feedback. Gipps (1995; Gipps and Stobart 1997) argues that feedback is a crucial feature of teaching and learning processes and one element in a repertoire of connected strategies to support learning. The chapters in this book reinforce the importance of feedback in enhancing the learning of individuals, groups and organisations.

In this chapter we explore and expand the discourses of feedback. We suggest that far from being a simple and uncomplicated notion, dilemmas and tensions arise when we talk and write about feedback. Feedback is a complex notion, often embedded in a common-sense and simplistic dominant discourse. In writing about feedback we find ourselves struggling with the conceptions and language in common use. Feedback is a term used in electronics, mechanics and ecology and these uses have an impact on its use in education. The feedback loop is familiar in electronic systems as high pitched whistling when sound output is returned to the microphone by a loudspeaker. In our central heating systems a thermostat relays information which results in the heating being turned on or off. Lovelock's mathematical model 'Daisyworld' demonstrated how temperature is regulated as a consequence of feedback loops between the ecosystem's organisms and their environment (Capra 1996). It is common to talk about 'giving' and 'receiving' feedback, but feedback is not always a 'gift' from one person to another. When there is a dominant discourse it is a struggle to find language which reflects alternative views.

This chapter briefly introduces the reader to the origins of the book and to its contents. It then sets out a framework for exploring different conceptions of feedback for learning. Each of these approaches is examined to consider how ideas about feedback are related to beliefs about learning, to explore the processes necessary for feedback to help learning and to identify some problems. We move on to consider how research paradigms influence beliefs about learning from research. The chapter concludes by suggesting that effective learning must include a wider conception of feedback than that of the dominant discourse and take on the characteristics of constructive and co-constructive dialogue described in this chapter and by many of the writers in this book.

ORIGINS AND SCOPE OF THIS BOOK

In *Feedback for Learning* we present multiple discourses on feedback. The book grew out of research seminars held at the Institute of Education, University of London, which gave the opportunity for members of the Assessment, Guidance and Effective Learning Academic group to present their research findings on feedback in a range of educational contexts. What emerged from the seminars was the importance of feedback in supporting learning at individual, group and organisational levels. We observed that a focus on feedback at all these levels is popular at the moment and that the notion of feedback seems generally to be taken as unproblematic. It also emerged that people had different perceptions of feedback, its functions and processes based on their perceptions of learning. These discourses are framed by the research interests of the contributors and do not cover the whole field.

Every chapter in the book is concerned with challenging the implicit assumptions on which approaches to feedback are based, and touch on a bigger question – what is 'effective' learning? The book explores feedback at different levels: Part 1 examines feedback in the classroom, Part 2 looks at feedback to teachers and Part 3 explores feedback at the organisational level.

A FRAMEWORK FOR ANALYSING FEEDBACK FOR LEARNING

Any evaluation of the usefulness of feedback must rest on an analysis of its purpose, the assumptions about learning on which it is based and a recognition that feedback has different purposes. Theoretical models help make common-sense assumptions about feedback explicit and open them up to analysis. Table 1.1 sets out three different models of teaching and related views of learning, and explores the goals which inform them: receptive-transmission; constructive; co-constructive.

THE RECEPTIVE–TRANSMISSION MODEL

This model of teaching and learning is described as receptive-transmission because these terms describe the states of the learner and the teacher. The teacher is an expert in a particular field and gives information to a passive recipient. In this model the curriculum is a body of worthwhile knowledge to which everyone is entitled (Hirst 1974), defined by the educational establishment, workplace or state. The transmission of this knowledge is the primary task of teaching, delivering concepts and facts. The curriculum content is non-negotiable, focuses on the cognitive and stresses the importance of rational thinking, that is objective, abstract, logical, sequential thinking. Dominant until the end of the 1950s, the receptive-transmission model still relates most closely to practice in educational establishments and accords with a mechanistic view of learning and organisations. A UNESCO report describes four kinds of essential learning: learning to know, learning to live together, learning to be and learning to do and suggests that educational methods currently pay disproportionate attention to the first type of learning (International Commission on Education for the Twenty-first Century 1996).

The failure to take an holistic approach to the educational needs of students is serious in a technological age. Knowledge soon becomes out of date. Young people need to be flexible, to make connections between their learning in one sphere and learning in another and to apply their

Table 1.1 Models of teaching, views of learning and related discourses on feedback

Model of teaching	Role of teacher and goals of teaching	View of learning	Feedback discourse
Receptive–transmission	• Expert • To impart new knowledge, concepts and skills	• Cognitive dimensions stressed • Learning is individual and affected by ability which is seen as fixed • Learning involves increased understanding of new ideas, memorising new facts • Practising new skills and making decisions based on new information	• Traditional discourse in which 'expert' gives information to others to help them improve • Primary goal to evaluate • Feedback is a gift
Constructive	• Expert • To facilitate discovery of new knowledge, concepts, skills • To help make connections, discover meaning, gain new insights	• Cognitive dimensions stressed, although social dimension recognised to some extent • Learning affected by ability which can develop and is affected by experiences • Learning involves making connections between new and old experiences, integrating new knowledge and extending established schema	• Expanded discourse in which 'expert' enables others to gain new understandings, make sense of experiences and make connections by the use of open questions and shared insight. • Primary goal to describe and discuss • Feedback as a two-way process (ping pong)
Co-constructive	• More equal power dynamic • Teacher is viewed and views himself or herself as a learner • To facilitate discovery of new knowledge, concepts and skills • To help make connections, discover meaning and gain new insights • To practise self-reflection and facilitate a reflexive process in others about learning through a collaborative dialogue	• The cognitive, emotional and social dimensions of learning are seen as inter-connected and equally important • The view of learning is extended to include reflection on the learning process itself and meta-learning (learning about learning)	• Expanded discourse involving a reciprocal process of talking about learning • Primary goal to illuminate learning for all • Feedback is a dialogue, formed by loops connecting the participants

learning to different situations. The model does not stress connections between different bodies of knowledge, between knowledge and personal experience. Indeed, it makes a distinction between the learner and what is to be learned (Prawat 1992). Emotional and social aspects of learning are not addressed and what the learner brings to the learning situation is unacknowledged or accorded no value. Consequently, issues of social justice or social transformation are not recognised or addressed.

This model fixes people in distinct roles. Learners are themselves divided according to perceptions of 'ability'. This in turn affects their perceptions of themselves as learners, for example, by disaffiliating them from the system of education. We know that teachers make early assessments of the ability of their pupils and 'ability differences are always apparently construed by teachers as stable' (Cooper and McIntyre 1996: 16). Those seen as successful in this model may be disadvantaged, as Hoffer suggests:

> In times of change learners inherit the earth, while the learned find themselves beautifully equipped to deal with a world which no longer exists.
>
> (Hoffer E. cited in MacGilchrist *et al.* 1997)

FEEDBACK IN THE DOMINANT DISCOURSE – THE GIFT

We characterise feedback in this model as a gift from the teacher to the learner. The teacher is viewed as expert in this discourse and feedback is one-way communication, from teacher to student, to provide information to help the student learn. The information is usually evaluative and may indicate the gap between current performance and desired outcomes.

Everyday use of 'feedback' is congruent with this dominant view of teaching and learning. It fits very neatly with the current educational policy discourse and therefore notions of feedback are popular at the moment. Educational priorities including target setting and performance management are based on a mechanistic, rationalist view of how to raise standards. They have in common a focus on external, rather than internal mechanisms for judging worth. They favour decision-making and critical judgement by others over self-reflection and self-awareness. They foster dependence rather than independence or interdependence and encourage notions of failure/success, wrong/right.

Current policy priorities do not foster an environment in which individuals or organisations are encouraged to risk making mistakes, to experiment or to be creative, the very things which are necessary for learning, development and progress (Seltzer and Bentley 1999).

We are familiar with feedback in this climate. It is given and received in many settings – solicited or not. Interview panels feel obliged to provide feedback to people who were not chosen for the job. OFSTED inspectors give verbal and then written feedback following an inspection of a school's performance. Mentors give beginner teachers feedback following observations of their performance in the classroom. Teachers and tutors give students feedback on draft assignments. Trainers ask for feedback following a course. Researchers provide evaluation reports for projects. Management training courses give advice on how to give 'positive' and 'negative' feedback and, more rarely, how to receive it.

In this discourse, feedback is a judgement about the performance of another. Feedback is given and received in the belief that the recipient will be able to adjust subsequent performances. It is assumed that the person giving the information knows more than the person receiving it, that the person receiving the information does not already know it, that they want to hear the information and this knowledge will lead to improvement. There is an expectation that feedback automatically leads to learning, but *how* learning can result from the gift of feedback is rarely considered problematic.

Feedback in the reception–transmission model can promote learning in some circumstances and with particular characteristics. Improvement is more likely to follow when part of a strategy which is understood by both teacher and learner (Clarke, this volume). The quality of the relationship between the giver and the receiver is significant in leading to learning (Carnell, this volume). Hargreaves, McCallum and Gipps (this volume) also explore effective ways of giving feedback within the dominant model.

Feedback which is intended to provide information and increase understanding is necessary when something is not for negotiation, when it is important to relate rules within a social context or social conventions regarding work and behaviour, and to indicate the consequences of not complying with conventions. But where we want to engage people in a deeper process of understanding, making connections, further insights or learning about their learning, this form of feedback is less effective.

We have coined the phrase 'killer feedback' to describe situations when the receptive–transmission form of feedback blocks learning.

Both authors have experienced receiving such feedback on writing. The feedback was intended to be constructive and developmental, but its effect was to discourage all further redrafting. This was because there was too much and it felt overpowering, it did not connect with our thinking at the time, there was no discussion or dialogue and it did not give any help in how to start making changes. It felt as if the person giving the feedback had their own purposes and goals for our writing.

In everyday use, positive feedback refers to judgements implying satisfaction with the learner's performance and negative feedback implies criticism and the need for changes. The recipient is assumed to welcome the former and the fear the latter. Our experience of killer feedback points to different conceptions of 'positive' and 'negative' feedback. We suggest that 'positive' feedback is only positive if it helps learning. The impact of positive feedback may be to motivate, for example, by increasing confidence, making new meaning, increasing understanding, helping to make links and connections. Negative feedback demotivates, for example, by discouraging, being overly judgemental, critical, giving unclear or contradictory messages and encouraging dependence on others for assessing progress. It is the experience of the recipient of the feedback which determines whether the gift is positive or negative.

So-called 'positive' feedback may prove to be unhelpful. Many teachers have a belief that praise forms an important function in motivating, rewarding and enhancing self-esteem. The review by Brophy (1981) indicates that giving praise in a general or indiscriminate way may be unhelpful, and may even lead to lower self-esteem and loss of confidence.

> Infrequent but contingent, specific, and credible praise seems more likely to be encouraging . . . than frequent, trivial or inappropriate praise. Rather than just assume its effectiveness, teachers who wish to praise effectively will have to assess how individual students respond to praise, and in particular, how they mediate its meanings and use it to make attributions about their abilities and about the linkages between their efforts and the outcomes of those efforts.
> (Brophy 1981: 27)

Feedback in the dominant model may also encourage comparison and competitiveness. The belief that comparisons between individuals encourage people to work harder to achieve their goals needs to be challenged. Comparison can lead to competition and may result in some individuals giving up, feeling they are failures and evaluating their abilities negatively. A review of research on formative assessment and learning recommends:

> Feedback to any pupil should be about the particular qualities of his or her work, with advice on what he or she can do to improve, and should avoid comparisons with other pupils.
>
> (Black and Wiliam 1998: 9)

One of the problems of the receptive–transmission model is that the person giving feedback can too easily become locked into stereotypes relating to gender, ethnicity, class and ability. Dweck shows how feedback in the receptive–transmission model can reflect the teachers' assumptions about girls and boys and their beliefs in their differing 'abilities'.

> Girls attributed failure to lack of ability rather than motivation; this was because teachers' feedback to boys and girls was such that it would lead to girls feeling less able, while allowing boys to explain their failure through lack of effort or poor behaviour. This reaction to feedback was only so for teacher feedback; peer feedback did not have this stereotypical effect.
>
> (Dweck *et al.* 1978, cited in Gipps 1995)

So far we have largely been discussing feedback given by 'experts' to others who are usually in a less powerful position. The dictionary definitions of feedback include 'information in response to an inquiry'. A different model of feedback which fits this definition is when the taught give information to the teacher in order for them to learn more about their professional practice. Teachers may ask for feedback from students at the end of a term or course. This book includes research with young people which sought to gather their views to feedback to their teachers about their careers education (MacDonald, this volume) and young people's feedback about how others support their learning (Carnell, this volume). The pupils' viewpoint should be highly valued because 'what pupils say about teaching, learning and schooling is not only worth listening to but provides an important – perhaps the most important – foundation for thinking about ways of improving schools' (Rudduck *et al.* 1996: 1).

As soon as we ask for feedback we open ourselves to the possibility of criticism – something which many of us find very difficult to handle. Despite these fears, adults often give feedback to young people which is highly critical. Feedback from the student challenges the dominant discourse since it shifts the balance of power and opens up the possibility of dialogue. It therefore moves in some respects towards the constructivist and co-constructivist models.

THE CONSTRUCTIVIST MODEL OF TEACHING AND LEARNING

In the constructivist model knowledge is constructed by the learner, including through activities such as participatory learning, open-ended questioning, discussion and discovery learning. Knowledge is related to the learner's everyday life and experiences. Those who support the constructivist model argue that teaching facts to people is ineffective unless they are taught how to construct their own schema for internalising the information and organising it so that it becomes their own (Costa 1991; Day 1981; Worsham 1988). These writers see the primary task of education as the development of thinking abilities for processing, acquiring and relating information to their own experience. A research study considered the teaching strategies which teachers and students found to be particularly powerful. These included group and pair work, story telling, use of stimuli which relates to pupil pop cultures, drama and role play, use of pictures and other visual stimuli. The researchers commented on the students' preferences.

> A powerful feature uniting all these preferred strategies was the opportunities they all provided for pupils to represent information in ways that they found personally meaningful.
>
> (Cooper and McIntyre 1996: 110)

In the constructivist model, it is accepted that young people have different intelligence levels and different talents, interests and skills. It assumes that young people are rational decision-makers, can be self-directed and learn autonomously. Learners are encouraged to make choices about their learning experiences, within limits placed on them by teachers and the school context. Education in this model is based on the principle of 'drawing out', rather than 'putting in'. The emphasis shifts from coercive approaches based on rules, regulation and punishment for infringements, to attempts to motivate pupils and develop their commitment to the values and norms of the organisation. It depends on the development of a relationship between teacher and student. The teacher has to be interested in finding out each learner's abilities, interests and skills. The constructivist model promotes the learning needs of individual children. In this model the cognitive dimension of learning is still dominant but there is recognition of the role played by social and emotional factors.

The increase in information has now outstripped our abilities to deal with it all in a lifetime. The need for greater information-processing skills has therefore received greater attention and the teacher's role has shifted to facilitator. This model developed in the 1960s and 1970s, based on egalitarian ideals of encouraging each child to achieve their maximum potential. It attempts to challenge some aspects of social injustice by providing the same educational opportunities for all, such as comprehensive schooling and 'mixed-ability' teaching.

FEEDBACK IN THE CONSTRUCTIVIST MODEL – PING-PONG

We have argued that in the dominant receptive–transmission model feedback is a gift, the transmission of more information to help the learner make improvements. In the constructivist discourse the purpose of feedback is to help make connections and explore understandings. Feedback in this discourse moves away from evaluative judgements. It becomes more of a description of the experience. In the dominant model feedback is given in 'you' language, in the constructivist model we are more likely to use 'I' language. This kind of feedback shares the giver's perceptions, rather than making generalisations or judgements. It is more likely to invite a response, to provide a narrative which can be added to, to offer insights for reflection. This approach to feedback has some features in common with counselling. The purpose of the feedback is to describe and discuss. We have used the term ping-pong to capture the to and fro of this discussion.

Although writers within the constructivist tradition have been interested in notions of empowerment and equality, we would argue that the power dynamic between those who give feedback and those who are on the receiving end has not shifted very far. Power still resides with the teacher, or with the evaluator, external researcher, or other expert because the agenda for the feedback is decided by them. Because the agenda is not decided by the person who 'receives' feedback, it may not be useful to them, or they may not know how to make use of it, as with feedback in the previous model. The teacher–learner dynamic is unchallenged.

Several chapters in this book describe how feedback given to an organisation such as a school, a group of teachers or an LEA by an outside researcher can generate discussion by providing data, and commentary on processes (Wikeley, Taggart and Sammons, and Thomas, Smees and Elliot, this volume).

THE CO-CONSTRUCTIVIST MODEL OF TEACHING AND LEARNING

The receptive–transmission and to a lesser extent the constructivist models reflect two dominant views of teaching and learning. We now introduce a third much less familiar model, the co-constructive model. This model has never become embedded in mainstream educational practice although individual teachers have incorporated some of the underlying principles into their practice. In this model there is a shift from a stress on individual responsibility for learning to a more collaborative view, allowing learners to identify issues in their organisation and society which affect their learning and well-being and then to act to bring about changes. Learning, in this model, involves reflective processes, critical investigation, analysis, interpretation and reorganisation of knowledge. Personal meanings and constructs are understood in their unique social and political context. Students produce work or solve problems that have meaning in the real world so that their work is intrinsically significant, not just proof that they can do well in school. As in the constructivist approach, this model represents a move towards a more systemic and less mechanistic view. This model is based on subjective reflection and action for change and incorporates the stages of the action-learning cycle (Watkins, this volume).

This model also incorporates meta-learning, that is learning about learning, the importance of which continues throughout life:

> The concept of learning throughout life thus emerges as one of the keys to the twenty-first century. It goes beyond the traditional distinction between initial and continuing education. It meets the challenges posed by a rapidly changing world. This is not a new insight, since previous reports on education have emphasised the need for people to return to education in order to deal with new situations arising in their personal and working lives. That need is still felt and is even becoming stronger. The only way of satisfying it is for each individual to learn how to learn.
>
> (International Commission on Education for the Twenty-first Century 1996: 22)

The role of the teacher in this process is to instigate a dialogue between and with their students, based on their common experiences. The role of the learner is to actively engage in the process. The relationships between teacher and learner are less hierarchical, boundaried and fixed than in the other two models. The goal of this model is to achieve enlightenment and empowerment through a process of individual, group and organisational change. This model of education is concerned with shifting the balance of power and working towards a fair and just society for all its members. Perhaps the best known proponent of this kind of approach is Freire (1990). Grundy describes it as follows:

> the emancipatory interest is concerned with empowerment, that is, the ability of individuals and groups to take control of their own lives in autonomous and responsible ways . . . At the level of practice the emancipatory curriculum will involve the participants in the educational encounter, both teacher and pupil, in action which attempts to change the structures within which learning occurs and which constrains freedom in often unrecognised ways.
>
> (Grundy 1987: 19)

It is difficult to conceive of this model being adopted in classrooms within the current UK educational climate, since the autonomy of teachers and educational establishments has been reduced and they are faced with increasing direction on what and how to teach. Students and teachers are expected to be less challenging and conform more. Aspects of this approach to teaching can be incorporated into classroom practice such as co-constructive dialogue between peers. This is often a feature of out-of-school learning (Carnell, Watkins, this volume). Involving parents in such dialogue is considered by Askew (this volume).

While this approach to learning may be rare in classrooms, it is more familiar to us in literature on learning organisations and learning communities. In the last ten years examples of such organisations, especially in the United States, have become available. When relationships between teachers involve this kind of learning, schools have been called 'professional communities'.

> Central to our idea of school-wide professional community is that collaboration is a generalised attribute of the school.
>
> (Kruse *et al.* 1995: 33)

Five characteristics of professional learning communities are suggested:

- shared norms and values;
- reflective dialogue;
- deprivatisation of practice;
- collective focus on student learning; and
- collaboration (Kruse *et al.* 1995).

The benefits of such communities are likely to be empowerment, personal dignity and collective responsibility for student learning in the face of scarce resources, uncertainty and lack of external rewards.

FEEDBACK IN THE CO-CONSTRUCTIVIST MODEL – LOOPS

In this model feedback is an integral part of the learning and better described as dialogue. The model draws on systemic thinking. As Senge says:

> in systems thinking, feedback is a broader concept. It means any reciprocal flow of influence. In systems thinking it is an axiom that every influence is both *cause* and *effect*. Nothing is ever influenced in just one direction.
>
> (Senge 1990: 75)

Feedback in this model is not a gift or batted back and forth within linear or hierarchical relationships, but constructed through loops of dialogue and information. As nothing is ever influenced in just one direction, responsibility for learning is shared. Feedback and reflection become entwined, enabling the learner to review their learning in its context and related to previous experiences and understandings – a 'meta' view which can lead to meta-learning.

Feedback, or dialogue, in this approach is much less concerned with judgements. Where it is understood that every part of the system interconnects, cause and effect are not considered so important. As a result, blame and criticism give way to problem-solving and extracting learning from the dialogue. The relationship is no longer one where the expert informs the neophyte of their judgement, but one where the roles of learner and teacher and shared and the expertise and experience of all participants are respected. All parties to such dialogues have an expectation of learning.

Such dialogues can emerge within all kinds of learning situations: between teachers (Watkins, this volume), in academic tutorial sessions, around the kitchen table, as part of school self-evaluation (MacBeath 1999), when teachers are reviewing their work, to improve organisational capacity for improvement (Reed and Stoll, this volume). What would it require to produce such dialogues between parents, students and teachers, researchers, inspectors and policy-makers?

FEEDBACK FOR LEARNING

Effective learning can be seen as a virtuous cycle, where effective learning promotes effective learning processes: the distinction between a process and an outcome decreases. Effective learning is usefully described in terms of its outcomes and its processes. Outcomes include:

• deepened knowledge;
• higher order skills, strategies and approaches;
• action towards greater complexity and more learning;
• positive emotions, excitement, enthusiasm;
• enhanced sense of self;
• more sense of connection with others;
• further learning strategies;
• greater affiliation to learning; and
• changed personal significance.

Effective learning involves processes such as:

• making connections about what has been learnt in different contexts;
• reflecting on one's own learning and learning strategies;
• exploring how the learning contexts have played a part in making the learning effective;
• setting further learning goals; and
• engaging with others in learning (Watkins *et al.* 1996).

We have argued that feedback in the receptive–transmission model is less likely to use these processes or to lead to these outcomes, whereas the co-constructivist approach, and to a lesser extent, the constructivist may involve many of the processes of effective learning.

In the receptive–transmission model learning will be in terms of increased knowledge, competence, skills, confidence and clarity about role in society (input–output model). In the constructivist model the change will be in terms of increased knowledge, competence, skills, autonomy, self-empowerment and clarity about role in society. Powerful arguments are being made for teaching and learning to take account of the needs of human beings now and in the future – what one writer tellingly calls 'permanent white water' (Vaill 1996). Some conceptions of learning may have been adequate for the 1950s and 1960s but they are no longer sufficient. Learners need to be effective learners, which includes learning about learning – meta learning (Askew and Carnell 1998; Watkins *et al.*, 2000)

FEEDBACK AND RESEARCH

The chapters which follow are based on research. In this chapter we have described different views of teaching which in turn relate to different epistemological positions, and we now extend this to include researchers' different perceptions of feedback. Epistemology is concerned with theories of knowledge and how it is acquired. The dominant view of teaching is congruent with an epistemological position that knowledge is external, to be discovered, has an objective reality.

> The dominant epistemology underpins most of mainstream education. This dominant epistemology, an analytical and objective way of knowing, does not tolerate experiential learning, action research, holistic medicine and other alternative ways of knowing and working.
>
> (Criticos 1993: 158)

Different epistemological positions underpin research and these are reflected in the views of feedback presented here. For example, in the chapter by Thomas, Smees and Elliot the researchers refer to their data as feedback which they provide for their clients. Other research paradigms view feedback in a way which is congruent with constructivist views of teaching and learning. For example, Wikeley's research raises the question of how teachers and researchers can use feedback to construct new understandings and make connections. Other forms of research, especially practitioner research, are congruent with the third concept of learning, co-construction. Knowledge is jointly constructed through dialogue. For example, Watkins (this volume) writes about how learning arises through dialogue between teachers.

READING THIS BOOK AND FEEDBACK

In this introductory chapter we have offered a framework of three conceptions of learning and feedback. We have explored these in the light of our understanding of effective learning, together with some of the tensions and difficulties with each of the models. We have particularly endorsed one model of feedback as effective in supporting learning – the dialogue. In considering the different models we have also referred to the research paradigms which inform the chapters and the authors' understandings.

We invite you, the reader, to consider how the chapters in this book relate to the framework we have offered, and to evaluate the framework's effectiveness. The subject of the book is feedback and so we also invite you to consider how useful this feedback about feedback is to you. However, there is an irony of which we are aware. The format of a book does not allow us to engage with our readers in the form of dialogue which we have endorsed.

REFERENCES

Askew, S. and Carnell, E. (1998) *Transforming Learning: individual and global change*, London: Cassell.

Biggs, J. B. and Moore, P. J. (1993) *The Process of Learning* (3rd edn), Englewood Cliffs, NJ: Prentice-Hall.

Black, P. and Wiliam, D. (1998) *Inside the Black Box: raising standards through classroom assessment*, London: School of Education, King's College, University of London.

Brophy, J. (1981) 'Teacher praise: a functional analysis', *Review of Educational Research* 51: 1, 5–32.

Capra, F. (1996) *The Web of Life: a new synthesis of mind and matter*, London: HarperCollins.

Cooper, P. and McIntyre, D. (1996) *Effective Teaching and Learning: teachers' and students' perspectives*, Buckingham: Open University Press.

Costa, A. L. (Ed.) (1991) *Developing Minds: a resource book for teaching thinking* (revised edition) (Vol. 1), Alexandria, VA: Association of Supervision and Curriculum Development.

Criticos, C. (1993) 'Experiential learning and social transformation', in D. Boud and D. Walker (eds) *Using Experience for Learning*, Milton Keynes: Society for Research into Higher Education and Open University Press.

Day, M. C. (1981) 'Thinking at Piaget's stage of formal operations', *Educational Leadership* 39: 1, 44–47.

Dweck, C. S., Davidson, W., Nelson, S. and Enna, B. (1978) 'Sex differences in learned helplessness: II The contingencies of evaluative feedback in the classroom and III, An experimental analysis' *Developmental Psychology* 14:3, 268–76

Epstein, D. (1993) *Changing Classroom Cultures: anti-racism, politics and schools*, Stoke on Trent: Trentham Books.

Freire, P. (1990) *Pedagogy of the Oppressed* (M. B. Ramos, Trans.), London: Penguin Books.

Gipps, C. (1995) *Beyond Testing: towards a theory of assessment*, London: Falmer Press.

Gipps, C. and Stobart, G. (1997) *Assessment: a teacher's guide to the issues* (3rd edition), London: Hodder and Stoughton.

Goleman, D. (1996) *Emotional Intelligence: why it matters more than IQ*, London: Bloomsbury.

Grundy, S. (1987) *Curriculum: product or praxis?* London: Falmer Press.

Hirst, P. H. (1974) *Knowledge and the Curriculum: a collection of philosophical papers*, London: Routledge and Kegan Paul.

International Commission on Education for the Twenty-first Century (1996) *Learning: the treasure within* (Report to UNESCO of the Commission, chaired by Jacques Delors), Paris: UNESCO.

Kruse, S. D., Louis, K. S. and Bryk, A. S. (1995) 'An emerging framework for analysing a school-based professional community', in S. D. Kruse, K. S. Louis and associates (eds), *Professionalism and Community: perspectives on reforming urban schools*, Thousand Oaks, CA: Corwin Press.

MacBeath, J. (1999) *Schools Must Speak for Themselves: the case for school self-evaluation*, London: Routledge.

MacGilchrist, B., Myers, K. and Reed, J. (1997) *The Intelligent School*, London: Paul Chapman.

Prawat, R. S. (1992) 'Teachers' beliefs about teaching and learning: a constructivist perspective', *American Journal of Education* 100:3, 354–95.

Rudduck, J., Chaplain, R. and Wallace, G. (eds) (1996) *School Improvement: What can pupils tell us?* London: David Fulton.

Seltzer, K. and Bentley, T. (1999) *The Creative Age: knowledge and skills for the new economy*, London: Demos.

Senge, P. M. (1990) *The Fifth Discipline: the art and practice of the learning organization*, London: Century Business.

Vaill, P. B. (1996) *Learning as a Way of Being: strategies for survival in a world of permanent white water*, San Francisco: Jossey-Bass.

Watkins, C., Carnell, E., Lodge, C., Wagner, P. and Whalley, C. (2000) *Learning about Learning*, London: Routledge.

Watkins, C., Carnell, E., Lodge, C. and Whalley, C. (1996) *Effective Learning*, London: University of London Institute of Education.

Whitaker, P. (1995) *Managing to Learn: aspects of reflective and experiential learning in schools*, London: Cassell.

Worsham, T. (1988) 'From cultural literacy to cultural thoughtfulness', *Educational Leadership* 46:1, 20–21.

Part 1

Feedback for young people's learning

2 Teacher feedback strategies in primary classrooms – new evidence

Eleanore Hargreaves, Bet McCallum and Caroline Gipps

INTRODUCTION

Feedback can be the vital link between the teacher's assessment of a child and the action following that assessment *which then has a formative effect on the child's learning.* The use of feedback is one means of making the function of assessments formative. Sadler (1989) suggested that if feedback does not have a formative effect on learning, then it is not truly feedback. What we mean by *formative* in this context, is that the pupil's learning strategies or understanding are formed into a more developed stage than they were prior to the particular assessment made.

In this chapter we are talking about feedback from the teacher to the pupil, in the primary classroom. We focus on verbal, non-verbal and written feedback that teachers give pupils. We depict different strategies teachers use to give feedback and we analyse the particular formative purpose that each strategy serves.

Recent research on teacher feedback in primary schools (Tunstall and Gipps 1996) has resulted in a feedback typology grounded in classroom practice. According to this typology, feedback can be evaluative, that is judgemental, with implicit or explicit usage of norms; or feedback can be descriptive, with specific references to the child's actual achievement or competence. Evaluative feedback can be positive or negative; descriptive feedback can relate to achievement or improvement.

In this chapter, we present new evidence about feedback in the primary classroom. In this research, we used Tunstall and Gipps' categorisations as our framework. This evidence comes from a two-year research project in which we looked in detail at teachers' teaching, assessment and feedback strategies in primary classrooms.

THE RESEARCH

The research on which this chapter is based was conceived in the early 1990s when teachers had been urged to operate in terms of a repertoire of teaching approaches and forms of pupil organisation (Alexander *et al.* 1992). It seemed important to us that feedback be seen as an integral part of the teacher's repertoire, through formative assessment. The aim of our study was to articulate a repertoire of *teaching, assessment and feedback* strategies for use in classrooms, building on formal theories of learning and the practice of good primary teachers.

The sample

From two Local Education Authorities we chose a purposive sample of 'expert' teachers based on the recommendation of Heads and senior advisers and using criteria negotiated with them. The research took place in twenty schools with twenty-three teachers (eleven Year 2 and twelve Year 6).

The timetable and methods

We visited our twenty schools in summer 1997 to interview the headteachers and observe lessons. In the autumn of 1997 we paid two-day visits to twenty-three teachers to observe up to three lessons in each classroom. Afterwards we carried out post-observation interviews and the Four Card activity. The Four Card activity involved teachers in a discussion about theories of learning.

In the spring of 1998, a further two-day visit was made to ten case study teachers where we observed two lessons in each classroom. During this visit teachers also took part in the Quote Sort activity for which they sorted fourteen quotes which focused on teaching, assessment and feedback strategies and on pupil learning. In summer 1998 we carried out the Quote Sort activity with the non case study teachers and finally, in autumn 1998, we held Focus Group interviews in both LEAs.

TEACHER FEEDBACK STRATEGIES IN PRIMARY CLASSROOMS

A wide repertoire of teaching, assessment and feedback strategies emerged from our analysis (see Gipps *et al.* 2000). In this chapter, the strategies that were dedicated to feedback are described in detail. We defined a feedback strategy as one where the teacher was 'imparting directly a judgement of a child, a child's strategies and skills, or a child's attainment (often in relation to goals) and giving information about the judgement'.

Teachers *presented* feedback to children in a range of ways. Feedback was given to individuals or to pairs and groups, or to the whole class. Feedback could be verbal, non-verbal, written, or a combination of these. In terms of the *contents* of feedback, it could be evaluative or descriptive, as categorised by Tunstall and Gipps' (1996) typology. The feedback strategies we explore in this chapter are the following:

- *Evaluative feedback strategies*
    - giving rewards and punishments,
    - expressing approval and disapproval.

- *Descriptive feedback strategies*
    - telling children they are right or wrong,
    - describing why an answer is correct,
    - telling children what they have and have not achieved,
    - specifying or implying a better way of doing something and
    - getting children to suggest ways they can improve.

THE STRATEGY OF GIVING REWARDS AND PUNISHMENTS

The giving of rewards and punishments was a form of evaluative feedback, in that explicit reference was rarely being made to the child's particular achievement. As rewards on written work, teachers drew or stamped smily faces, gave stickers or other stamps, stars, merits or house points. They might give these rewards as they praised the child in interaction. Other rewards included being applauded by the rest of the class, being invited to write on the blackboard or being awarded extra time on the computer.

Punishments were less obvious, and consisted of the withholding of rewards in many cases, or the removal of rewards such as a deduction of house points. One teacher gave un-smily faces and one teacher tore up work that was not worthy of the child. Children were moved away from friends, and told to work through their lunch time or do extra homework, if they were not working efficiently.

Rewards were used to motivate children in the sense of encouraging them to keep learning and trying, to think, *'I've done well here'*. Teachers believed that rewards could raise children's self-esteem and so spur them on. Punishments were used to reduce the likelihood of a recurrence of undesirable performance.

Several teachers did, however, display an awareness of the negative impact that both rewards and punishments could have on pupils' learning.

THE STRATEGY OF EXPRESSING APPROVAL AND DISAPPROVAL

As with other feedback strategies, the strategy of expressing approval and disapproval could be verbal, non-verbal or written. Non-verbal strategies of expressing approval included the teacher nodding, making eye contact, smiling, laughing, putting an arm around or patting the child and taking on a mild manner in order to be approachable. Non-verbal means of expressing disapproval included pulling faces, staring hard, clicking fingers or making disapproving noises. Verbal expressions of approval included praise phrases such as 'Well done', 'Good boy/girl', 'Brilliant'. Verbal expressions of disapproval included such criticisms as 'Don't talk rubbish!' The expression of approval and disapproval was a form of evaluative feedback in that often its purpose was approval or disapproval of the child himself or herself: the teacher implied that she felt that work was 'Excellent' or 'Disappointing', but without relating this evaluation to specified achievement criteria.

Teachers offered praise for correct answers, for good work, for using a good method, for effort and for independent thinking. Disapproval was most commonly expressed in relation to behaviour, although this was often learning behaviour: when children argued, were not listening, or were not concentrating.

At least eleven teachers (six from Y2), considered the expression of approval to be a means of showing the child that he or she was valued. Expressions of approval functioned to encourage children to continue working; to move on to the next stage of their work; to want to contribute in class; to be willing to find things out; to take risks; or to work independently. One teacher commented that, *'the more motivated the child, the easier it is to get that child to want to learn for itself'*.

Fifteen teachers stressed the importance of giving negative as well as positive feedback, although a few teachers felt that younger children needed less negative feedback than older children. One Y6 teacher admitted she would sometimes be honest and say it was '*a really dreadful piece of work*'. Negative feedback served to make a future occurrence less likely.

Several teachers recognised that evaluative feedback which showed their approval or disapproval, needed to be accompanied by descriptive feedback that explained why an answer was right or good or how it might be improved. For example, one teacher said:

> *there is no point in you praising a child, patronising them and saying this is wonderful, this is good, all the time, when really and truly they don't know what's good about whatever it is, they haven't been given any pointers or tips of how to improve.*

THE STRATEGY OF TELLING CHILDREN THEY ARE RIGHT OR WRONG

The first stage towards describing to a pupil what is good or less good about his or her achievement, may involve the teacher feeding back to the child whether a response is right or wrong. Our research showed that a simple way of telling children they were wrong, was for the teacher to say 'No', and perhaps to turn to someone else for the right answer. Teachers could feed back to children that they were wrong by demonstrating, themselves: one teacher was seen to use a child's suggestions in using a measuring scale, already knowing they were incorrect, to allow the child to see for himself that they would not work.

We observed that sometimes teachers fed back that an answer was incorrect by putting a question to the child, either repeating an original question or posing a new one. For example, one Y6 teacher read out a limerick and asked the class to find a word to rhyme with 'Bengal'; one boy said, 'party', and the teacher did not say 'No' but asked him why he had said party and then asked what other rhymes were in the poem. We observed that some teachers invited the child to reread a question or redo his or her own answer. A few teachers, however, stressed to children that there was no 'right' or 'wrong' way and that all contributions from them were valuable.

On written work, an incorrect response might be indicated by the use of a cross, dot or underlining, or an empty box where the child could write the correct answer. In all subjects we observed, crosses to indicate a wrong answer were less common than ticks to indicate a correct one.

Teachers told children that they were right, often by simply saying 'Right', 'Yes' or 'Spot on!' or they might nod or smile instead. An evaluative phrase of praise, such as just saying 'Thank you', was a similar means. A common strategy was for the teacher to repeat the child's correct verbal response; some teachers consolidated this by then writing it on the blackboard or asking the child to do so. We observed a few teachers who fed back when a response was correct through a question, for example by asking a pupil to explain her response in more detail because it was exactly right. On written work, ticks were a common means of showing a child that his or her response was right.

The function of this strategy was to sort the correct from the incorrect. Teachers told children that their response was right or good to confirm attainment of a desirable outcome. One Y2 teacher felt that this helped children *'to know what's acceptable and what would be a good idea to do'*. The function of telling a child he or she was wrong was to indicate which areas the child needed to concentrate on.

Teachers could only feed back to children that they were right or wrong if they had already made some assessment. This assessment could be of the whole class or of an individual. The function of this feedback strategy was to confirm attainment or to pinpoint an area of weakness, following assessment, in order subsequently to enable improvement in a specific area.

THE STRATEGY OF DESCRIBING WHY AN ANSWER IS CORRECT

We observed teachers as they described what was good about their achievements to children and noted that this description was often accompanied by an evaluative phrase of praise. For example, a Y6 teacher said to one child, but in front of the whole class, *'Good girl! You've used "freckly" and "polished" which is a very good description of the top side of leaves'*. Teachers sometimes described why the work of the whole class was good, not just an individual within it.

With regard to written descriptions of why an answer was correct, we observed a comment for some creative writing, *'Well written, lots of detail and good vocabulary'* and for science, *'Good, you have carefully compared the two rocks'*. These were in contrast to evaluative comments which were not accompanied by description, such as simply, 'Well done' or 'Good'.

Teachers used one child's correct response to teach the class, by explaining to the whole class why the one child's response was good. For example, a Y6 teacher announced to the whole class that one boy had used the word 'decreased' instead of 'gone down', which was an achievement in his use of mathematical language. Teachers therefore used this feedback strategy in order to confirm a child's achievement, but also to inform children about acceptable performance. In this way, pupils learnt what they should produce again, but also learnt how to extend their achievement towards further progress.

At least five teachers directed children specifically to look at the comments they had made on their written work. On the other hand, at least four teachers felt that written comments needed to be used with caution, since some children had difficulty in reading them.

THE STRATEGY OF TELLING CHILDREN WHAT THEY HAVE ACHIEVED AND HAVE NOT ACHIEVED

In using this strategy, teachers told children how far they had met pre-specified learning intentions or formal targets, worked within time targets or even achieved National Curriculum levels.

Ten teachers, seven of them from Y6, described how they summed up what had, and also what had not, been learnt in a lesson, in relation to learning intentions. One teacher described the summing up as the *'sharing of what we intended to do and what actually has happened'*. At the individual level, one Y6 teacher summarised for a child, *'Yes. You have found two words that mean "house"'*. And a Y6 teacher presented a 'Got it!' stamp to anyone who seemed to have grasped a specified concept well.

At least ten teachers told children what they had or had not achieved in relation to targets. These were targets which had been achieved or targets which they set for the child, in order to clarify where the child needed to progress to next. Teachers described clearly to the child what these targets represented. For example, if the target was Level 4 in writing, then the teacher described the criteria represented by Level 4 in writing. Time targets were another kind of target: at least five teachers stressed to children what they should achieve within a set time limit.

The function of this strategy was to inform the child what he or she had learnt in relation to a specific goal, and what he or she still had not learnt, in relation to a specific goal. The intended outcomes of using this strategy were: to celebrate a child's achievements; to motivate children by showing them how far they had already come; to clarify to children where they were aiming; to order targets in their heads; and to consolidate or reaffirm whatever had been learnt. One Y6 teacher described how:

> *It's helpful to them to give a brief summary, overview of what they have done, to put all that knowledge and information into some sort of order in their heads: 'Why have we been doing it? What have I learnt? Oh yes, that's what I learnt.'*

THE STRATEGY OF SPECIFYING OR IMPLYING A BETTER WAY OF DOING SOMETHING

We observed teachers specifying or implying to children how they could improve a piece of work or a skill. By its nature, this type of feedback was descriptive. It was Y2 teachers who stressed the role of discussion as a vehicle for specifying or implying a better way of doing something, while it was the Y6 teachers who felt it was useful to write specific details in children's exercise books, about doing something a better way.

We observed teachers advising children to begin a task again. Five teachers described re-demonstrating or re-explaining a task for the child to try anew, thus specifying a better way of doing the task. For example, one Y2 teacher in a handwriting lesson wrote the first letter in a row of the same letter, where the child had written her own row incorrectly.

Teachers also pointed out what was missing in children's work or skills, while recognising what was not missing first. Six teachers said they might advise the children to try a specific exercise or method or to practise a particular skill. For example, in a creative writing lesson, a Y6 teacher advised the class to concentrate on 'technical' skills. Another Y6 teacher suggested to her pupil that she use a dictionary to help her spell.

In some cases, the teacher commended the child's own response, and then showed how it could be even better. In other cases, the teacher modelled a correct answer, demonstrated how to do a task or provided an alternative to show the child how to improve, sometimes asking the child to compare his or her own performance with the teacher's example. Three teachers described writing out spellings or handwriting patterns for children to practise.

The function of the strategy was to enable pupils to do better. Teachers specified or implied a better way of doing something in terms of showing a pupil how to make specific corrections, how to meet a newly set target or how to move forward towards a more extended achievement.

THE STRATEGY OF GETTING CHILDREN TO SUGGEST WAYS THEY CAN IMPROVE

Teachers used this strategy by asking individuals to feed back to them ways they could improve. In order to get children to suggest (or describe) ways in which they could improve, teachers used commands, such as 'Go back and check your work'; invitations, such as 'Tell me how . . . '; or questions, such as 'What would make this better?' At least five teachers asked children to relate the improvement to a target, and some teachers invited children to set their own targets. We observed one Y2 teacher who did this on a regular basis (although sometimes she made suggestions for the child), writing the suggested targets at the front of each child's mathematics, science and English exercise books. For other teachers, it was less formalised. A Y6 teacher explained,

> *I may talk to them individually and say to them, 'What do you want to do next?' or 'How could you now go and improve this work?' I probably wouldn't actually call it a target.*

In these ways, teachers asked children to say what was right or wrong in their work, why their work was correct or incorrect, how it could be better, or to describe next steps towards achieving a target not yet met. This type of feedback was therefore necessarily descriptive.

Twelve teachers, five from Y2, told us that, through this strategy, they invited children to be self-critical. A Y6 teacher explained,

> *sometimes I ask them to go back and look at what they did wrong and see if they can correct it and I always say, 'Do you know why you made that mistake?'*

At least twelve teachers, six from each of Y2 and Y6, tried to get children to discuss ways they could improve so that their thinking was challenged. A Y2 teacher explained she would be

> *talking to them about what they had done and, by questioning processes, I'd be able to move them on and ask, 'So what if . . . ?' or 'How could you move this on?' or 'How could you change that in order to make it better?'*

NEW EVIDENCE

The research described in this chapter provides new evidence of a repertoire of teacher feedback strategies. The following annotated, verbatim transcript illustrates the strategies in use and authenticates our observations of the strategies in an actual lesson.

> A Year 2 teacher is touring the room, checking children's handwriting practice.
> (*T* = teacher, *C* = child)

T. Hang on a minute, Chelsea. These Ts need to be a bit taller because the top needs to go up to there. [Telling a child she is wrong]
Good boy, Declan! Yes, you've got your Ps in the right place. [Expressing approval; telling the child he is right; and describing why an answer is correct]
That's lovely, Lauren. [Expressing approval]
Well done, Robbie. [Expressing approval]

C. There you are.

T. Yes, well done. P, Q . . . Now, this one with the capital R. Let's have another look at this. If you look at mine up there, it's more like this one. What's the difference? What's the difference? [Getting the child to suggest ways she can improve]

C. That bit.

T. Yes, this bit, his head, needs to be all the way up to the top. [Specifying a better way of doing something] If not, what letter does he look like?

C. K.

T. K. [Telling a child she is correct by repeating her answer]
There is some beautiful handwriting this morning. [Expressing approval; telling children what they have achieved]

FEEDBACK FOR LEARNING

Within the suite of strategies described in this chapter, a gradual shift is perceptible. With evaluative feedback, as in expressing approval and disapproval, the teacher has all the control in feeding back to the child. At the other extreme, as in getting children to suggest ways they can improve, the child takes the initiative and provides feedback to himself or herself, only supported by the teacher.

In part, teachers' choice of feedback strategies depends on their beliefs about how children learn. Most teachers in our research held the view that children learnt by building on what they already knew, by asking and being asked questions and by making connections. Many also believed that children learnt by discovering for themselves. These views might lead the teacher to choose any or all of the descriptive feedback strategies, particularly those whereby the pupil takes responsibility for his or her own learning and improvement. Some teachers believed that children learnt when the teacher transmitted information (on occasions, at least), which might lead teachers to choose strategies of telling children they are right or wrong and describing why an answer is right or wrong. All teachers also held that how the child felt about himself or herself affected learning, and they therefore chose evaluative strategies in an attempt to boost children's motivation and self-esteem.

We conclude, therefore, that depending on how teachers perceived learning to come about, and what sort of learning they hoped to encourage, teachers used a repertoire of feedback strategies in order to bring about transformation in learning. And this repertoire was closely interrelated to the repertoires of assessment strategies as well as teaching strategies, that they also used.

REFERENCES

Alexander, R., Rose, J. and Woodhead, C. (1992) *Curriculum Organisation and Classroom Practice in Primary Schools*, London: Department of Education and Science.

Gipps, C., McCallum, B. and Hargreaves, E. (2000) *What Makes a Good Primary School Teacher: expert classroom strategies*, London: Falmer.

Sadler, D. (1989) 'Formative assessment and the design of instructional systems', *Instructional Science* 18, 119–144.

Tunstall, P. and Gipps, C. (1996) 'Teacher feedback to young children in formative assessment: a typology', *British Educational Research Journal* 22:4, 389–404.

3 Getting it right – distance marking as accessible and effective feedback in the primary classroom

Shirley Clarke

INTRODUCTION

The chapter begins with a reminder of the current demands of the National Curriculum and other contextual requirements, then refers to firm research evidence on the impact of formative assessment. Research about feedback and marking is then explored in order to establish classroom conditions for success. Finally, I describe the effects of my own intervention research in which teachers were asked to put into place some practical strategies, based on the theory, for making distance marking a more accessible and effective form of feedback.

FEATURES OF THE CURRENT CONTEXT

Teachers in England are statutorily obliged to teach the content of the National Curriculum, a key aspect of which sets out large numbers of learning objectives for each of ten subjects. Since 1993 schools have been inspected under the framework of the Office for Standards in Education. Current practice in inspection includes asking children what the learning intention of a lesson is. The 'Literacy Hour' began for primary age children in 1998, and the Numeracy Strategy began in 1999. Both Literacy and Numeracy Strategy specify learning objectives derived from the National Curriculum statutory coverage. Although it is not statutory, schools have to have equivalent quality in their teaching of English and high statutory test results if they are to avoid the pressures of being involved. This framework sets out a very detailed teaching programme and precise timings of lessons. The content of the Literacy curriculum is reflected in the focus of this chapter: many issues of marking are illustrated in relation to prose or narrative writing. Since the onset of this initiative an issue for feedback has emerged:

teachers feel there is no time for oral feedback because of the pressure of content.

RESEARCH EVIDENCE ABOUT FORMATIVE ASSESSMENT

Black and Wiliam's (1998a, b) significant review of the impact of formative assessment made clear what was going wrong in English schools and what needed to happen to enable children to be more successful learners. The Assessment Reform Group (1999), a group of academics who commissioned the review, have since proposed some implications for practice and policy in *Assessment for Learning: beyond the black box*. The following selections set the scene for this chapter:

> The research indicates that improving learning through assessment depends on five, deceptively simple, key factors: the provision of effective feedback to pupils; the active involvement of pupils in their own learning; adjusting teaching to take account of the results of assessment; a recognition of the profound influence assessment has on the motivation and self esteem of pupils, both of which are crucial influences on learning; the need for pupils to be able to assess themselves and understand how to improve. (p. 4)

This was further broken down to include:

> sharing learning goals with pupils, involving pupils in self assessment, providing feedback which leads to pupils recognising their next steps and how to take them, underpinned by confidence that every student can improve. (p. 7)

The inhibiting factors identified included:

> A tendency for teachers to assess quantity of work and presentation rather than the quality of learning; greater attention given to marking and grading, much of it tending to lower the self esteem of pupils, rather than to provide advice for improvement; a strong emphasis on comparing pupils with each other which demoralises the less successful learners; teachers' feedback to pupils often serves managerial and social purposes rather than helping them to learn more effectively. (p. 5)

Within the context of these findings and the need to find practical strategies with which to apply them, this chapter explores the role of the teacher in distance marking and describes some attempts to turn the theory into practice.

EXPLORING THE RESEARCH IN ORDER TO FIND PRACTICAL STRATEGIES

Definitions of teacher feedback and their relationship to distance marking

Closing the gap

Ramaprasad (1983) defined feedback as 'information about the gap between the actual level and the reference level of a system parameter which is used to alter the gap in some way'. Sadler (1989), writing about formative assessment, simplified this by establishing three conditions for effective feedback to take place:

> The learner has to
> a) possess a concept of the *standard* (or goal, or reference level) being aimed for,
> b) compare the *actual* (or current) *level of performance* with the standard, and
> c) engage in appropriate *action* which leads to some closure of the gap.
>
> (Sadler 1989)

Sadler comments on Ramaprasad's definition of feedback as follows: information about the gap between actual and referenced levels is considered as feedback *only when it is used to alter the gap.*

With this framework of the teacher's role, the control lies entirely with the teacher. The teacher defines the goal, judges the achievement and tries to close the gap between achieved and desired performance. The findings of Black and Wiliam (1998a, b) emphasise the importance of the involvement of the child of such assessment, so we need to be careful not to oversimplify the process, leaving the child with no stake in the process. Although children and teachers can set their own learning goals, the all-encompassing statutory demands of the National Curriculum present a huge number of 'must cover' learning objectives. At best, control for the teacher and the child lies in the application of the goal, how it is broken down into mini-goals, process and attitude goals, the judgement of how far it has been reached and in finding strategies with which to close the gap. This chapter focuses mainly on what the teacher can do first in modelling the process of marking, thus training children to be able to contribute to the marking process.

Tunstall and Gipps (1996), in their discussion about feedback, referred to Pollard's (1990) social-constructivist model of the teaching/learning process, in which the teacher is the 'reflective agent', providing 'meaningful and appropriate guidance and attention to the cognitive structuring and skill development arising from the child's initial experiences'. The child is thus supported in the process of 'making sense' of the learning and is helped to cross the 'zone of proximal development'. It is often the case that, instead of giving specific, concrete strategies to help children move from what they have achieved to what we want them to achieve, teachers instead simply reiterate the desired goal. For example: 'You need to give a better description here' merely reiterates the learning goal of 'write a descriptive story opening'. Better advice would be that which focuses on how to improve the description, for example: 'What was the prince wearing?', 'Could you describe just the prince's face?'.

For distance marking (that is, where the only form of individual feedback a child receives is via the words and marks made on the work by the teacher) it seems that several conditions need to apply to establish an effective model of feedback from teacher to child. Children need to know the learning intentions of the task and then how far they have fulfilled them. In terms of the learning intention, children then need to be shown what they could have achieved, or where to go next. Advice about spelling, handwriting and so on should not be mentioned for every piece of work, or children will be overloaded with information. Finally, they need to be shown how to 'close the gap' between current and desired performance. 'Shown' in this context would ideally include an invitation to include the child's perceptions and strategies.

Focusing on learning intentions

A significant feature of effective feedback in many studies is the importance of informing children of the learning objective of a task (e.g. Ames and Ames 1984; Hillocks 1986; Butler 1988; Crooks 1988). Sadler (1989) stated that 'hard goals have the greatest impact on performance', compared to 'do your best goals'. Butler (1988) elaborated on this through her studies involving goal orientation. She found that information about performance that focuses attention on the learning

objective of a task (e.g. 'These three adjectives are very effective'), promotes task involvement and high subsequent interest. In contrast,
information that focuses attention on the self (e.g. 'You worked very
hard on this') promotes ego-involvement and lower subsequent interest. Ames and Ames (1984) found that competitive task orientation
(e.g. public charting of progress, attainment grades) focuses children on
how clever they are compared to their peers, whereas task mastery systems (perceptions of the present goal relative to one's prior
achievements) focuses children on the task.

How teachers have given written feedback to children about their writing

The purpose of marking children's work appears to be clear: it provides
valuable personal feedback to children about their performance and
related improvement. However, the traditions of marking have often
been in conflict with this definition. Chater (1984) found that the main
purpose of marking in primary schools was for the teacher to have a
written record and that teachers were greatly affected by the quality of
handwriting. If good handwriting is a key requirement for all work, the
message is clear to children: the priority goal orientation must be good
handwriting, with other goals taking a secondary focus. Further studies have revealed that primary teachers are more interested in quantity
rather than quality and adherence to learning objectives (Bennett *et al.*
1992). Tunstall and Gipps (1996) observed that teachers' feedback on
children's work was either evaluative (judgemental – concerned with
affective aspects) or descriptive (task related – cognitive) and Bennett
and Kell (1989) found that, although teachers often explained the task
in cognitive terms (e.g. 'I'm looking for how well you can order
the mixed up pictures of the story'), their assessments of children's
performance were often presented in affective terms (e.g. 'You have
worked very hard') Sadler (1989) suggested that it is easier for a
teacher to comment on effort and the degree of expertise than concepts
mastered and facts learnt.

Hargreaves and McCallum (1998) found that teachers often specified attainment and indicated improvement, but rarely against the
learning intention of the task. The traditional culture of marking seems
to take over at this point, where teachers almost automatically see
marking as a process of mainly indicating errors related to surface features of the writing, through red pen marks, and making improvement
suggestions through prose at the end of the work. Feedback from
teachers indicates that there is an expectation that the more teachers

write in children's books, the better they appear to have been doing their job. There is also the very significant parental expectation that children's work should be marked in this way. Zellermayer (1989), however, found that most children ignore comments written on their work; if they do read them the comments are often misunderstood. Cohen (1987) also observed that the 'learner's repertoire of learning strategies is often too limited to process many of the comments'. It seems that we need to look more closely at the purpose, content and viability of marking if it is to provide feedback to children which can be understood and used.

Models of excellence

Zellermayer's article (1989) concludes 'Learning writers need positive response that is specific and relates to what their instruction has focused on.' The importance of carrying the learning intention through to the feedback stage is emphasised here, as well as the need to be focused and specific when giving feedback. This implies that teachers should ignore certain errors in children's writing and only give feedback about *those aspects the child was asked to pay attention to.*

Tunstall and Gipps' (1996) work on teacher feedback to young children resulted in a number of categories to describe the types of feedback teachers engage in, including 'specifying attainment' and 'specifying the way forward'. If we combine this definition with Zellermayer's conclusion and Sadler's emphasis, we can construct a useful practical definition of effective feedback for marking: *the teacher must give feedback against the focused learning objectives of the task (whatever the child was asked to pay attention to), highlighting where success occurred against those objectives and suggesting where improvement might take place against those objectives.* Taking account of Sadler's advice that we need to help children to 'close the gap', indicating improvement needs is not enough. *We must give appropriate prompts or strategies to enable children to make those improvements.*

MY RESEARCH: AN INTERVENTION APPROACH TO MARKING

Over several years of action research, the theoretical background was applied through my work with hundred of teachers attending ongoing INSET courses at the Institute of Education. The courses all dealt with formative assessment, breaking it down into sharing learning goals, self-evaluation and feedback, including marking. Teachers' shared practice was used as a starting point, then the most successful strategies trialled by all in the group each time. Teachers' best practice was then the starting point for the next course with new teachers. Each course led to further development of the practical strategies while maintaining the research underpinning (Clarke 1998). The most recent effective practical strategies for distance marking and their impact are drawn from the experiences of those teachers, as well as my own school-based observations and interviews with teachers and children. The focus was distance marking rather than work marked with the child present.

The practical strategies

1 Make sure the learning objective of a task is secure. These are derived from the National Curriculum programmes of study, the QCA Schemes of Work, the Literacy or Numeracy objectives or teachers' own breakdowns of the statutory objectives.
2 Tell children the learning objective of every task, both orally and by displaying it. Make it explicit. If appropriate, include success criteria as well as the learning intention.
3 Focus the distance marking on the learning intention of the task, by highlighting, say, three parts which have best fulfilled the objective and inserting an arrow where improvement against the learning intention could take place. By the arrow, write a 'closing the gap' prompt to help the child know how to improve this part.
4 Mark spelling etc. only if the child was asked to pay attention to those things *after* they had first attended to the learning objective rather than *at the same time*. The emphasis here was that the arrow should *not* indicate spelling errors and so on, but only where improvement could take place in terms of the learning intention of the task.
5 Avoid writing large sections of prose at the bottom of children's work, which might not be understood.
6 Allow a few minutes of specific lesson time for children to read the marking and make the improvement of the arrowed part, using the 'closing the gap' prompt as a guide.

Findings

The impact of sharing learning intentions

Positive feedback:

- It forces the teacher to be more focused on the learning intention rather than the activity.
- It sharpens the teacher's understanding of the learning intention.
- Children are more likely to express their learning needs (e.g. 'I would like to work on my own in order to do learn this'/'I would find a number line easier' etc.).
- A learning culture develops in the school, as children start to use the language of the learning intentions rather than the language of the activities.
- The quality of the work improves: in the amount done, in the adherence to the learning intention and success criteria of the task, in children's ability to produce their best.
- Children persevere for longer at a task.
- Children are more focused at beginnings of lessons.
- Children have greater ownership of the lesson, as responsibility for the learning is shifted from the teacher to the child.
- Teacher expectations rise.
- Behaviour improves.
- Children are put into an automatically self-evaluative position when given the success criteria.
- Stating learning intentions makes a plenary or subsequent reflection against the learning intention a necessity.

Negative feedback:

- It can be difficult to make the learning intention explicit if it is too broad.
- It takes time to get into the habit.
- The success criteria can become a reiteration of the task instructions rather than what the teacher wants to see by the end.
- It takes practice to realise that all learning intentions can be tackled in this way, whether they are open or closed. For instance, a learning intention focused on investigative science would need to be given the success criteria of as 'What I'm looking for is that you can find a way of finding out what effect exercise has on the heart'. Initially, some teachers worry that the investigation will be invalid because they will have 'given the game away' and told the children what the end result should be.

Quotes from children included the following:

She writes the learning intention on the board for every lesson and it's very useful. You know what to concentrate on and what to aim for. It's really improved. Before I was trying to do everything and now I concentrate on just what I need to. (Upper ability Year 6)

It's made it clearer – I can just look on the board and know what to concentrate on. (Middle ability Year 4)

Children's self-evaluation occurred naturally in some schools, where teachers used A4 paper on the white board, tearing them off each time to fall on the floor after each lesson. Children became interested in the pile of learning intentions and how much they had learnt that day. Teachers have capitalised on this interest by co-ordinating class discussions about what has been learnt throughout the day, or setting up individual self-evaluation journals for children to complete at the end of the week. In some cases, teachers have started to display a timetable for the week's learning intentions (not the activities) at the request of the children.

The impact of the focused marking (highlighting success and improvement against the learning intention with a 'closing the gap' prompt)

Conditions for the approach to work well were as follows:

- The learning intentions need to be the foundation of the marking, both for the children and the teacher.
- Teachers need to organise a class session, with children's work on acetate, where the teacher goes through the highlights and arrows in order to familiarise the children with the approach.
- Spellings and other features are best checked by the children after they have finished their work, so that they only focus on one or two things at a time, then the teacher can mark what the children have already checked.
- Where the task is closed (i.e. wrong or right answers), there is nothing to be gained over ticks and crosses, although arrows and closing the gap prompts can still apply.

Some examples of highlights against success, arrows and prompts for improvement are shown in Figures 3.1 and 3.2.

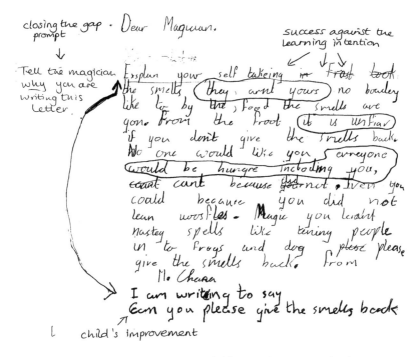

Figure 3.1 Learning intention (Year 4 child): to write a persuasive letter

The 'closing the gap' prompt comments

Understanding about the 'closing the gap' prompts developed as teach-ers applied the strategy and found that many children were still not able to make an improvement because the prompt comment was too broad. Three ways of writing the closing the gap prompt were found:

1 A reminder prompt (often enough for brighter children), such as 'How do you think the dog was feeling here?'.
2 A scaffolded prompt, such as 'What do you think the dog's tail was doing?'.
3 An example prompt, such as 'Choose one of these phrases or one of your own: the dog was very surprised/the dog couldn't believe his eyes/the dog wondered what had happened'.

The example prompt was seen as the most successful, often with all but the brightest children, especially in Years 3 and 4. One of the out-comes of this approach was that children often decided on their own

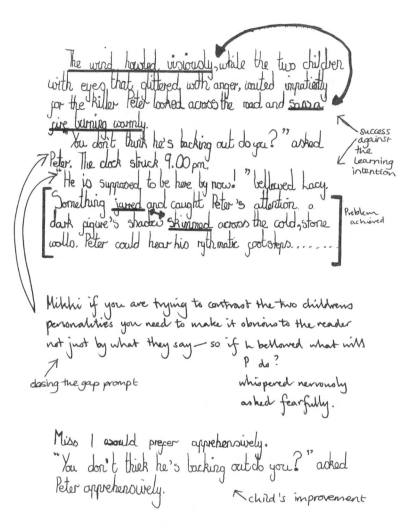

The wind howled visiously, while the two children
with eyes that glittered with anger, waited impatiently
for the killer Peter looked across the road and saw a
fire burning warmly.
    "You don't think he's backing out do you?" asked
Peter. The clock struck 9.00 pm.
    "He is supposed to be here by now!" bellowed Lacy.
[Something jarred and caught Peter's attention, a
dark figure's shadow skimmed across the cold, stone
walls. Peter could hear his rythmatic footsteps.......]

success against the learning intention

Problem achieved

Mikhi if you are trying to contrast the two childrens
personalities you need to make it obvious to the reader
not just by what they say — so if h bellowed what will
P do?

closing the gap prompt

whispered nervously
asked fearfully.

Miss I would prefer apprehensively.
"You don't think he's backing out do you?" asked
Peter apprehensively.

child's improvement

Figure 3.2 Learning intention (Year 6 child): to write a story opening which uses contrast

word or phrase if given some examples. The modelling of examples appears to encourage children to think of their own improvement more easily. The same results occurred with mathematics and science work.

Positive feedback:

- It cuts down the marking time required for the teacher.

- It is liberating to focus mainly on the learning intention.
- The highlights and arrows make the marking accessible for children, so the time needed to read and act on it is less than marking as comments.
- The approach further emphasises a learning rather than an activity culture.
- The approach works well when marking with a group.
- Children appear to enjoy the highlights and making the improvement.
- Creating the 'closing the gap' comment makes the teacher have to think about the exact needs of the child – tailoring the comment gets at the heart of being a teacher.
- The approach can be used effectively when marking with children.
- Children made clear improvements.
- The process is very supportive for children with special needs as it boosts self-esteem.
- It focuses the teacher on the purpose of marking, being to give feedback to children.
- Self-evaluation is improved: children are able to look for their own highlights and arrows after time.
- Focusing on one thing leads to more obvious improvement in their repertoire of skills.
- Paired marking with the strategy is very constructive.

Negative feedback:

- If the prompt is unclear the children do not improve and can become demoralised.
- It is hard to change long-established habits of marking spelling and so on for every piece of work.
- Creating the 'closing the gap' comment makes the teacher have to think about the exact needs of the child – tailoring the comment gets at the heart of being a teacher, so takes time to get right.
- It can be difficult to decide which pieces of work will be marked in this way, because you want to mark everything.

As well as recognising that the purpose of marking was for the teacher to give feedback to the child, quotes from children included the following:

I think it's made a difference to my learning, because you get to know what you're supposed to be doing and then how to make it even better. (Upper ability Year 5)

It's important to actually do the improvement on your work. If you just read what the teacher said and didn't do the improvement you wouldn't be able to do it again in other work. (Middle ability Year 4)

CONCLUSION

Distance marking has always been a poor substitute for oral, face-to-face marking, because it relies on the child being able to make sense of words and marks alone. However, the research about feedback and marking shows that, even if marking is understood, it has more impact on children's progress if it is focused against learning intentions and suggests explicit strategies for improvement. Time management of marking is another burden for teachers, which, with a more focused approach, as discussed here, can be eased. The use of codes (e.g. highlights over words, phrases or calculations and arrows with prompt comments) to highlight success and improvements against learning intentions fulfils two functions: it makes the feedback more accessible to children than prose (as long as they are sure of the meaning of the codes) and makes marking less time-consuming.

Although Zellermayer (1989) stated that the critical implication of his studies was that 'written feedback is not sufficient for writing instruction', the advent of the National Curriculum and the Literacy Hour in England has made distance marking in primary schools more common than ever before, in the struggle to give children feedback before the next lesson. In secondary schools, distance marking is the main form of individual feedback students receive. It seems timely, therefore, that we continue to investigate ways in which we can challenge traditional marking practice and improve the ways in which we give feedback to children through the written word and the marks we make on their work.

REFERENCES

Ames, C. (1992) 'Classrooms: goals, structures, and student motivation', *Journal of Educational Psychology* 84:3, 261–271.

Ames, C. and Ames, R. (1984) 'Systems of student and teacher motivation: toward a qualitative definition', *Journal of Educational Psychology* 76:4, 535–556.

Assessment Reform Group (1999) *Assessment for Learning: beyond the black box*, Cambridge: University of Cambridge School of Education.

Bennett, N. and Kell, J. (1989) *A Good Start? Four year olds in infant schools*, Oxford: Basil Blackwell.

Bennett, S. N., Wragg, E. C., Carre, C. G. and Carter, D. G. S. (1992) 'A longitudinal study of primary teachers' perceived competence in, and concerns about, national curriculum implementation', *Research Papers in Education* 7:1, 53–78.

Black, P. and Wiliam, D. (1998a) 'Assessment and classroom learning', *Assessment in Education* 5:1, 7–75.

Black, P. and Wiliam, D. (1998b) *Inside the Black Box: raising standards through classroom assessment*, London: King's College.

Butler, R. (1988) 'Enhancing and undermining intrinsic motivation; the effects of task-involving and ego-involving evaluation on interest and performance', *British Journal of Educational Psychology* 58:1, 1–14.

Chater, P. (1984) *Marking and Assessment in English*, London: Methuen.

Clarke, S. (1998) *Targeting Assessment in the Primary Classroom*, London: Hodder and Stoughton.

Cohen, A. D. (1987) 'Student processing of feedback on their composition', in A.L. Wenden and J. Rubin (eds), *Learner Strategies in Language Learning*, Englewood Cliffs, NJ: Prentice Hall International.

Crooks, T. J. (1988) 'The impact of classroom evaluation practices on students', *Review of Educational Research* 58:4, 438–481.

Hargreaves, E. and McCallum, B. (1998) *Written Feedback to Children from Teachers*, ESRC Project 'Teaching, Assessment and Feedback Strategies' (work in progress) Project paper No. 7, London: University of London Institute of Education.

Hillocks, G. (1986) *Research on Written Composition: new directions for teaching*. Urbana, IL: National Conference on Research in English.

Pollard, A. (1990) 'Towards a sociology of learning in primary schools', *British Journal of Sociology of Education* 11:3, 241–256.

Ramaprasad, A. (1983) 'On the definition of feedback', *Behavioural Science* 28, 4–13.

Sadler, D. (1989) 'Formative assessment and the design of instructional systems', *Instructional Science* 18, 119–144.

Tunstall, P. and Gipps, C. (1996) 'Teacher feedback to young children in formative assessment: a typology', *British Educational Research Journal* 22:4, 389–404.

Zellermayer, M. (1989) 'The study of teachers' written feedback to students' writing: changes in theoretical considerations and the expansion of research contexts', *Instructional Science* 18, 145–165.

4 Dialogue, discussion and feedback – views of secondary school students on how others help their learning

Eileen Carnell

INTRODUCTION

This chapter examines three forms of communication around support for learning: dialogue, co-operative discussion and teacher to student feedback. These emerged from analysis of interviews conducted with secondary school students. The aim of the research was to investigate young people's perceptions of how others help their learning. The chapter analyses young people's experiences and discusses these in relation to associated perceptions of learning.

Key issues emerge. Different forms of communication are seen as helpful to support learning but their appropriateness and impact are dependent on the contexts in which they occur, learning goals and the nature of young people's relationships with teachers and peers.

My research for the past six years has focused on effective learning (Carnell 1999). For this study I interviewed fourteen students in twos or threes in the same year groups (seven to eleven) but from different form groups. I began each interview by asking them to describe a recent occasion when someone helped them with their learning. Interestingly, all examples were about verbal communication. I was struck by the different examples the young people chose, including occasions in and out of school, with teachers, other students, friends and family.

I begin the analysis with the young people's examples of dialogue. I then examine co-operative discussion. Finally I explore teacher to student feedback. Within each section I consider some ideas about the associated model of learning and some constraints in practice. To set the scene I include a summary of each.

The main features of dialogue are that people engage together in talk to enhance their learning. It is informal conversation, open-ended, spontaneous and occurs outside the classroom. People learn collaboratively, share responsibility for learning and work towards mutual goals. Learning is seen as complex, multi-dimensional and involving all. Dialogue transforms relationships and encourages actions for change. The young people are responsible for their actions and time. Co-operative discussion appears similar to dialogue but there are crucial differences. Both co-operative discussion and dialogue involve working together through conversation but co-operative discussion involves less commitment to joint goals (Oldroyd and Hall 1992). In the examples young people offered, the goals are set by the teacher. The location is always the classroom. In co-operative discussion the style is formal and controlled. The teacher either manages the occasion or takes overall responsibility.

Teacher-to-student feedback is characterised by one-way communication. The teacher is seen as the expert and provides information to the student about their work, to clarify goals, to identify mistakes or provide advice. In the examples, feedback was sometimes used to help develop understanding and take thinking forward. Teacher-to-student feedback takes place in classrooms under the control of the teacher.

DIALOGUE

Dialogue seems to occur in particular contexts and is characterised by the informality and spontaneity of the occasion. Young people said dialogue did not happen in lessons but after school, at lunch-time or at home.

It was particularly striking that dialogue was never managed by the teacher, although once was initiated by the teacher:

> We had to give in course work for a certain week. There was a deadline. So the teacher suggested we come in to help each other. We gave each other ideas, suggestions and stuff, asked for opinions, 'Is it good?', 'Is it alright?'. It was after school so everyone felt more free like. The teacher didn't say anything to us if we walked about the classroom and normally when you are in school you have to stay in your seat. (Year 11 Male)

The characteristics of dialogue are equality, sharing, spontaneity, collaboration and reciprocity. What I found interesting is that young people do not think such experiences are appropriate for the classroom where a particular view of behaviour is perceived:

> After school classes are the tops. Yea, you do it better. After school they [the students] don't mess about, they just get on with their work helping each other. I have never heard a teacher in class say to talk to each other about your work. They never say that do they? In class they say get on with your work and work on your own. (Year 11 Male)

As Brookes and Brookes suggest, 'Dialogue is not a tile in the mosaic of school experienced by most students' (Brookes and Brookes 1993: 108).

Dialogue allows learners greater control and responsibility for learning rather than relying on the teacher. Through practice self-directed learners develop:

> I remember one occasion when we had homework to do and none of us had done it and we all got together in the library, maybe ten or twelve of us. We all missed our lunch. Someone would look this up and someone would look that up and everyone worked together and we got it done. If you work on something with a whole group of friends I think that is much more better than doing it with a teacher. Everyone got the best out of it because we were dedicated to it and got the best answers by working together and talking and sharing. (Year 10 Female)

This situation is more like a collaborative learning community where learning is shared and socially constructed. This may be termed co-construction. Co-construction is grounded in the assumption that learners are teachers and teachers are learners. Hierarchies are broken down, boundaries less evident and responsibility shared. The following quote illustrates this point:

> We had to think of a plot by ourselves and I couldn't think of anything and my Mum and my Mum's boyfriend and a neighbour all sat in the kitchen and they all started arguing and that helps me learn. Like it is one-to-one, no really it's more than that. In the classroom it is with one teacher with a load of students but at home it is like so many teachers and just me as part of it. I think it is much better. In the classroom you can just fade away into the background. You can sit there and do a bit of work or not. But if you are in a situation with your family you can't possible sit there and not be part of what's going on. There were a lot more ideas than you would get in class.

Q. Does this sort of conversation happen in lessons?
No way. You are expected to behave differently in class. You have to sit up straight and wait for your turn with the teacher. (Year 10 Female)

Theorists of group interaction differ as to how explicit and rational discourses should be for productive small groups (Cohen 1994). The social constructivists have documented how groups negotiate meaning moment by moment (see Cohen 1994). Other writers see effective learning as an explicit strategy in which groups must manage the process of problem solving with conscious planning and execution of tasks. In these examples of learning outside the classroom, meaning appears to be constructed moment by moment. This is characterised by spontaneity, which appears to be less evident in classroom interactions:

> If I was discussing my ideas with the teacher then I'd feel that I was pushed for time and the whole point of talking with the teacher would be just to get the work done. At home it is just like a conversation.
> Q. How is it different?
> With a teacher they have got an aim of what they want you to come up with. But if you are talking just generally about one thing that leads on to talking about another thing, then something completely different. My Granddad walked in and then he said something else that no one had thought of and it just took off. I was learning so much from all the different points of view. (Year 10 Female)

These examples indicate how learning in informal settings can be more engaging than classroom learning. These findings have similarities with other research reviewed by Resnick (1987) (see Table 4.1).

Table 4.1 Learning in and out of school

In school	Out of school
Learning is usually	Learning is usually
• decontextualised	• contextualised
• second-hand, may need motivating	• first-hand, may come easily
• individualistic	• co-operative
• assessed by others	• self-assessed
• structured formally	• less structured

In formal learning situations the greatest premium is placed upon 'pure thought' (Resnick 1987: 13). In less formal contexts there is a less-boundaried view. Informal, contextualised environments are more relevant to the needs of today's learners (Gardner 1991).

In interviews where young people were discussing 'out of school' dialogue it was striking that grades and performance never featured; there was more emphasis on learning and understanding. In the examples of classroom learning there seemed to be emphasis on grade-related performance and achievement.

The relation between dialogue and learning

Dialogue is more than conversation. It can be seen to build learning-centred narrative. As Senge (1990) reminds us, the original meaning of dialogue is the sharing of ideas and meaning, to enable insights not attainable individually. Boyd (1996) puts it like this: 'coming together in conversation creates something larger than both of us' (Boyd 1996 cited in Anderson 1999).

The term suggests more commitment to learning. Dialogue requires:

- presence – a willingness to follow the conversation as it leads in 'unrehearsed' directions;
- unanticipated consequences;
- vulnerability;
- temporal flow – sensitivity to time – past, present and future; and
- authenticity – a presumption of honesty. (Anderson 1999)

The following definition is helpful in understanding the relation between dialogue and learning. Dialogue is:

> a dynamic generative kind of conversation in which there is room for all voices, in which each person is wholly present, and in which there is a two-way exchange and criss-crossing of ideas, thoughts, opinions and feelings. Likewise, learning and the development of knowledge is a dynamic generative process.
> Transformation occurs in and through dialogue, and intrinsically, relationships transform. (Anderson 1999: 65)

Transformation is key. Dialogue is likely to bring about change as it invites complex learning. Change may not be in relation to behaviour but in relation to change in perception of experiences – a change in the way one sees oneself in relation to others.

CO-OPERATIVE DISCUSSION

In the interviews with young people two forms of co-operative discussion emerged: teacher managed and student initiated. The following examples show how teachers manage co-operative discussion in the classroom:

> Sometimes we are put in groups to do the work set. It involves talking. We talk till the teacher says stop. The teacher tells two people to speak to another two and then you have to say what they tell you to two other people to see if you really understand what it is about. (Year 8 Male)

> Sometimes the teacher gets us to move the tables and then we work in a circle. We discuss our learning and then we all understand what is going on. It helps because when we don't understand we hear what others have to say and it is more better. (Year 7 Male)

In these examples we see a shift in the role of the teacher from 'knowledge expert' to 'learning manager' which has advantages for teachers and students. Co-operative discussion in the classroom embodies democratic principles by:

- making pupils' frames of reference central;
- freeing the teacher from an authority-based role;
- enabling more open communication and shared meaning;
- allowing openness and negotiation of change; and
- endorsing the existence of social relationships among students and teachers and offering the chance for more personal encounters (Salmon and Claire 1984). This can only happen in an atmosphere of trust and support.

The following examples show how co-operative discussion in the classroom may be initiated by the young people themselves:

> When I am sitting next to my friend and they are ahead of me and I'm stuck they help me out by talking about it. If I am trying to work it out or if I can help my friend who is stuck then we help each other. (Year 8 Male)

> Working with others gives you a chance to discuss the work you are doing. It gives you an opportunity to get better grades in your work without the teacher's help. (Year 8 Male)

These are examples of what Cohen (1994) describes as routine types of learning. Students help each other understand what the teacher or textbook is saying and provide substantive and procedural information. The interactions are different when the objective is learning for understanding or conceptual learning:

> Working in a small group in class is really helpful. You hear everyone's ideas and you can say 'No he doesn't agree with me and why not?' And 'She does', and 'She is sort of halfway'. It is really good because you understand what you think compared with other people's views. (Year 10 Female)

This illustrates a mutual exchange process in which ideas, hypotheses, strategies and speculation are shared (Cohen 1994).

Effective co-operative interaction

Co-operative discussion requires social interdependence (Abrami *et al.* 1995). That is, the necessity for group members to depend on each other for their learning. This also applies to dialogue, but co-operative discussion in the classroom places more emphasis on structure, planning and tasks. Cohen (1994) hypothesises that only where there are group tasks which require social interdependence, will interaction result in learning gains. For task groups to be effective in the classroom there are two requirements – collective action and reciprocal interdependence (Cohen 1994). The young people I spoke with were aware of the difficulties when the interaction was characterised by one-way dependence:

> You need to be good workers where you each put the same amount of effort in, otherwise one person would do all the work and the other one nothing. (Year 10 Female)

In order to overcome one-way dependence task instructions need to ensure 'resource interdependence' or 'goal interdependence' (Cohen 1994).

Abrami *et al.* (1995) use the term 'promotive interaction' to include communicating effectively through positive social interdependence, providing mutual help, building trust and managing conflict. The relationship between interdependence and interactions is bi-directional: 'Co-operation promotes trust, trust promotes co-operation, greater co-operation results in greater trust' (Abrami *et al.* 1995: 32). In such a climate there is no room for competition. Competition:

- can lead to severe discouragement for students who have few academic successes;
- discourages students from helping each other;
- encourages the cover up of misunderstandings;
- threatens peer relationships;
- tends to segregate groups into higher or lower achieving students;
- discourages intrinsic motivation; and
- tends to encourage students to attribute success and failure to ability, rather than effort (Gipps 1995).

I was interested to see that on the only occasion where competition was mentioned it was related to achieving higher grades:

> In every lesson I work with others but I get a better grade. I want a better grade than the persons I work with. (Year 8 Male)

I was struck by the number of times young people talked about their work in relation to improving grades, even in co-operative settings. This appeared to be linked to a motivational style to do with performance rather than learning. This is most usefully illustrated by Dweck's research (1986) on motivational styles (see Table 4.2).

Table 4.2 Different motivational styles and their characteristics

Performance orientation	*Learning orientation*
• Belief that ability leads to success	• Belief that effort leads to success
• Concern to be judged as able and to perform	• Belief in one's ability to improve and learn
• Satisfaction from doing better than others or succeeding with little effort	• Preference for challenging tasks
• Emphasis on interpersonal competition and public evaluation	• Derives satisfaction from personal success at difficult tasks
• Helplessness: evaluates self-negatively when task is difficult	• Applies problem-solving and self-instructions when engaged in tasks

People with a learning orientation can talk themselves through the difficulties they meet, including difficulties in a learning process (Watkins *et al.* 1998). Handling freedom, open-ended situations, and different interpretations, needs to be learnt (Askew and Carnell 1998).

TEACHER-TO-STUDENT FEEDBACK

The third form of communication offered by young people in the interviews was teacher-to-student feedback. This form of communication:

• clarifies goals

> If the teacher gives you suggestions I think that's very good because it will help give you a goal so you have something to work towards. (Year 9 Female)

• gives a sense of direction and purpose

> Teachers are trying their hardest to make us learn. Teachers are giving us suggestions. It helps us know where we are going. (Year 8 Male)

• identifies mistakes

> When you have finished a piece of work it is good when the teacher corrects you and tells you your mistakes. (Year 11 Male)

• provides advice

> Teachers' comments give you something to work with. You know how you can get good grades. (Year 10 Female)

Importantly, the extent to which feedback had an impact depended upon the nature of the relationship between the young person and their teacher. This was commented on many times, for example:

> It is not helpful to have a one-to-one with a teacher you don't know well because you really feel pushed. But if you talk with someone else about your learning, someone who you know really well then that is better, you learn more 'cos you trust them. If the teacher is really bothered then it is different. (Year 10 Female)

Mutual understanding and influences are liable to distortion if honesty and a predisposition to accept and accommodate others' views and feelings are absent. The following quote demonstrates this misconception:

If the teacher puts it bluntly then you can really take offence, Oh No, I've got to do it all over again. The teacher doesn't like it and I got a 'D' and I got it all wrong and I'll have to do it all again. (Year 10 Female)

Young people are aware of how teachers can take offence. They are sometimes wary of being open:

You can talk to friends more better. With friends you don't hesitate, you can say whatever you want – things that just come out of your mouth. You feel more free. When you speak to a teacher you have to be careful you don't say the wrong thing in case he or she will take it the wrong way. (Year 11 Male)

You can't say 'I don't really understand any of this whatsoever' because the teacher would say 'What? We've been doing this for three weeks. What's going on?' (Year 10 Female)

These quotes underline why feedback may remain a one-way process from teacher to student. Discussion is not invited.

Teacher-to-student feedback: its relation to learning

The above examples illuminate the most commonly held view of feedback in school – the process of passing information in one direction from teacher to learner. Gipps (1995) suggests that in this view of feedback, teachers use their judgements about the learner to feed back into the teaching process. This determines whether to:

- give further practice on it;
- help learners move to the next stage;
- confirm correct responses; or
- tell learners how well the content is being understood, and identify and correct errors – or allow the learner to correct them.

In this view of feedback, the correction function has been seen as probably the most important aspect (Gipps 1995). In this view, feedback is seen to have three elements – the desired goal, evidence about present position, and some understanding of a way to close the gap between the two (Sadler 1989) (see also Clarke, this volume). This perspective may be problematic especially as the goals are set by the teacher. The goals may not be clear to the learners:

Some teachers, they don't define what we are doing, they don't go further. And then when we are talking because we don't know what we are supposed to be doing they say well if you get bad results that is your fault it ain't my fault. (Year 11 Male)

Here it appears that the teacher is not sharing the goals or checking that the goals are understood. This causes problems for the student and leads to misconceptions on both sides.

The language used by the young people illustrates a particular form of communication, for example, 'the teacher *gives* suggestions', '*tells* you your mistakes', '*makes* us learn'. This form of feedback reflects a reception view of learning in which teacher 'instructs' their pupils. The reception view assumes:

- the learner is an empty vessel;
- the teacher transmits knowledge;
- learners learn what they are taught (Gipps 1992).

In this view, feedback is considered important for two reasons. It contributes directly to progress in learning through the process of formative assessment. It contributes indirectly through its effect on pupils' academic self-esteem (Gipps 1995).

An alternative form of teacher feedback to students reflects a different view of learning. In the construction view of learning, as opposed to a reception view, the teacher provides meaningful and appropriate guidance and extension to the learners' experiences. This supports learners' attempts to 'make sense' of their experiences and enables them to cross 'the zone of proximal development' – a spectrum of achievement attainable only with support (Vygotsky 1978). The young people I spoke to gave examples of how the teacher is expected to do this:

If you are in a group and someone is trying to help you but they don't know any more than you, you are covering the same sort of ground. It is not going to help because you are at the same level, so the teacher has to help you. It is good for revision if you are at the same level, but not for real learning.
Q. What do you mean 'real' learning?
Well, um, it takes you further, you know more and you understand more. (Year 10 Female)

In another interview one said:

A teacher telling you what to improve on is unhelpful. There is a difference between a teacher who tells you and a teacher who gets you to think about it and understand it so you can work out how you understand it. (Year 9 Female)

Here we see feedback taking a different form. The emphasis is on understanding and clarity. The construction view assumes:

• learners actively construct knowledge for themselves;
• knowledge derives from interactions; and
• learners determine their own knowledge (Biggs and Moore 1993).

More complex views of feedback reflect more complex views of learning. Such views stress feedback as a crucial feature of the teaching–learning process (Gipps 1990; 1995). There is growing recognition of the importance of feedback as part of the formative assessment process in enhancing effective teaching and learning (Gipps 1995; Black and Wiliam 1998a, b). In practice this means less use of teacher feedback for evaluative or grading purposes and more use of teacher feedback about the processes of learning (Crooks 1988), what one young person described as 'real learning'.

Others stress putting learning at the core of all assessment activities, involving the learner more as a partner (Gipps 1995; Black and Wiliam 1998a, b). In a learning partnership, learners can take responsibility for their 'performance' and monitor their learning, whatever their age (Gipps 1996). This change to become learning partners is part of a paradigm shift in approaches to feedback which are about making learning more effective. This perspective introduces self-regulated learning, meta-cognition (thinking about thinking) (Gipps 1996) and meta-learning (learning about learning) (Watkins *et al.* 1996; 1998).

Some classroom dilemmas

The idea of a learning partnership with a teacher did not arise during these interviews. It did seem possible, however, in other contexts:

My Dad's best friend really helped me. I worked with him for a long time. Even though the teachers are really good they sort of just put it in your head. They do explain it to you, but when you know the person better and when you are outside school and you don't sort of have to be sitting up straight and listening, you are able to relax. They casually explain it to you and you can talk back and compare it with what you think and it is much more helpful. (Year 10 Female)

The crucial difference between 'putting it in your head' (the reception model) and an alternative model based on constructing knowledge in a partnership, seems to be about the amount of time it takes to develop such relationships, the informality of the context and a particular view of learning. Classrooms are busy places (Doyle 1983; 1990) and in situations where teachers are attempting to maintain control, they may curtail the potential for pupil participation and discussion (McNeil 1986). As one put it:

> I sometimes sit down and work on my own, I sometimes work with others, I sometimes ask the teachers for help. It depends. I am not worried about getting a higher grade. I am more interested in getting a good reputation.
> Q. A good reputation?
> Just to sit down and get on with your work quietly and not run around the classroom. (Year 8 Male)

This is an example of a strategic learner (see Ertmer and Newby 1996) who uses their knowledge about themselves and about the task or context requirements to deliberately select strategies to achieve the desired goal. In this case this learner selects a superficial approach to learning to match context expectations. Views about appropriate classroom behaviour were commented upon several times as being a significant factor in inhibiting learning.

A SUMMARY AND CLOSING THOUGHTS

Following this analysis of the three forms of communication that support young people's learning I present a summary (see Table 4.3).

Our perceptions of learning, the learner and the learning context have a direct impact on how we work in the classroom.

Peer learning requires learner responsibility which restructures power relationships; relationships are non-hierarchical. At first, teachers and learners may be uncomfortable with the redistribution of responsibility (Abrami *et al.* 1995). Students may too; the required shift from accepting and compliant student to influencing and responsible learner needs practice and support. Seeing ourselves as teachers

Table 4.3 Characteristics of dialogue, co-operative discussion and feedback

	Dialogue	Co-operative discussion	Teacher to student feedback
Context	Out of school	In school	In school
Relationships	Non-hierarchical Teacher seen as learner, learner as teacher	Hierarchical Teacher and learners' roles boundaried	Hierarchical Teacher and learners' roles boundaried
Purpose/function	Change in the perception of experience	Development of understanding	Clarification, direction, correction
Approach to learning	Self-directed, commitment to joint goals	Teacher-directed	Teacher-directed
Focus/orientation	Learning orientation, emphasis on learning and understanding	Performance orientation, emphasis on grades and attainment	Performance orientation, emphasis on grades and attainment
Model of learning	Co-construction collaboration	Construction co-operation	Reception/ transmission
Communication	Bi-directional	Two-way	Mainly one-way
Structure	Spontaneous, informal and open-ended	Planned, formal and controlled	Planned, formal and controlled
Responsibility	Shared among learners	Individual/shared with teacher	Individual/teacher

who 'help students to search rather than to follow is challenging and, in many ways, frightening' as it involves a shift from 'a well-managed classroom to a transformation seeking classroom' (Brookes and Brookes 1993: 102–103). Teachers need support from colleagues to work in different ways in the classroom. These research findings may be threatening for teachers if the dominant discourse in school is one-way teacher to student feedback. A paradigm shift is needed to encourage learning dialogue both among teachers and students and between teachers and teachers. Given support teachers engage with such extensions to their current practice readily (see Watkins, this volume).

These research findings suggest the possibility that as young people acquire a view of themselves as active participants in their own learning, they then become more committed and effective as learners.

REFERENCES

Abrami, P., Chambers, B., Poulsen, C., De Simone, C., D'Apollonia, S. and Howden, J. (1995) *Classroom Connections: understanding and using cooperative learning*, Toronto: Harcourt Brace and Company.

Anderson, H. (1999) 'Collaborative learning communities', in S. McNamee and K. Gergen (eds) *Relational Responsibilities: resources for sustainable dialogue*, Thousand Oaks, CA: Sage Publications.

Askew, S. and Carnell, E. (1998) *Transforming Learning: individual and global change*, London: Cassell.

Biggs, J. B. and Moore, P. J. (1993) *The Process of Learning*, Englewood Cliffs, NJ: Prentice Hall.

Black, P. and Wiliam, D. (1998a) 'Assessment and classroom learning', *Assessment in Education 5*: 1, 7–75.

Black, P. and Wiliam, D. (1998b) *Inside the Black Box: raising standards through classroom assessment*, London: King's College, School of Education.

Boyd, G. (1996) *The A. R. T. of agape listening: the miracle of mutuality*, Sugarland, TX: Agape House Press.

Brookes, J. G. and Brookes, M. G. (1993) *In Search of Understanding: the case for constructivist classrooms*, Alexandria, VA: Association for Supervision and Curriculum Development.

Carnell, E. (1999) 'Understanding teachers' professional development: an investigation into teachers' learning and their learning contexts', unpublished PhD thesis, Institute of Education, University of London.

Cohen, E. G. (1994) 'Restructuring the classroom: conditions for productive small groups', *Review of Educational Research* 64:1, 1–35.

Crooks, T. J. (1988) 'The impact of classroom evaluation practices on students', *Review of Educational Research* 58:4, 438–481.

Doyle, W. (1983) 'Academic work', *Review of Educational Research* 53:2, 159–199.

Doyle, W. (1990) 'Classroom knowledge as a foundation for teaching', *Teachers' College Record* 91:3, 347–360.

Dweck, C. (1986) 'Motivational processes affecting learning', *American Psychologist* 41:10, 1040–1048.

Ertmer, P. A. and Newby, T. J. (1996) 'The expert learner: strategic, self-regulated, and reflective', *Instructional Science* 24:1, 1–24.

Gardner, H. (1991) *The Unschooled Mind: how children think and how schools should teach*, New York: Basic Books.

Gipps, C. (1990) *Assessment: a teachers' guide to the issues*, London: Hodder and Stoughton.

Gipps, C. (1992) *What We Know about Effective Primary Teaching*, London File, London: Tufnell Press.

Gipps, C. (1995) *Beyond Testing: towards a theory of assessment*, London: The Falmer Press.

Gipps, C. (1996) *Assessment for the Millennium: form, function and feedback*, London: Institute of Education, University of London.

McNeil, L. (1986) *Contradictions of Control: school structure and school knowledge*, New York: Routledge and Kegan Paul.

Oldroyd, D. and Hall, V. (1992) *Development Activities for Managers of Collaboration*, Bristol: University of Bristol, NDCEMP.

Resnick, L. B. (1987) 'Learning in school and out', *Educational Researcher* 16:9, 13–40.

Sadler, D. (1989) 'Formative assessment and the design of instructional systems', *Instructional Science* 18, 119–144.

Salmon, P. and Claire, H. (1984) *Classroom Collaboration*, London: Routledge and Kegan Paul.

Senge, P. (1990) 'The leader's new work: building learning organisations', *Sloan Management Review* 32:1, 7–23.

Vygotsky, L. S. (1978) *Mind in Society*, Cambridge MA: Harvard University Press.

Watkins, C., Carnell, E., Lodge, C., Wagner, P. and Whalley, C. (1998) *Learning about Learning*, Coventry: NAPCE. [also London: Routledge, 2000]

Watkins, C., Carnell, E., Lodge, C. and Whalley, C. (1996) *Effective Learning: Research Matters No 5*, London: University of London Institute of Education School Improvement Network.

Part 2

Feedback for teachers' learning

5 Feedback between teachers

Chris Watkins

In this chapter I describe the orientation and common practices I have met when working with teachers who are offering each other feedback in a range of school settings. After analysing these practices, the assumptions underlying them and their shortcomings, I propose three extensions to current practices and offer some impressions on their use.

For the last ten years a proportion of my work has been with teachers mentoring other teachers in four main contexts: experienced teachers with beginner teachers, colleagues mentoring newly qualified teachers, general mentoring in a school for newcomers and those new in role, and experienced headteachers mentoring new headteachers (Watkins 1992; 1997a, b; Watkins and Whalley 1993; 1995). Although some teachers accentuate the differences between these four roles, I see significant similarities in the relationships which are developed. I have also been involved in staff development for appraisal, and have worked with schools interested in paired learning for teachers. In this chapter, if I use the term mentor, I do not intend to allude to the formal aspects of schemes, rather to a teacher who is engaged in supporting the learning of another teacher. And if I use the term 'learner teacher' I mean any teacher at any point in their life/career.

CURRENT CONTEXT: AN ORIENTATION TOWARDS PERFORMANCE EVALUATION

In the contexts I meet, a pervasive orientation emerges which influences the content and practice of one teacher 'giving feedback' to another. This orientation is highly evaluative as though the role of the person giving feedback was to judge the performance of the other and somehow pass on that judgement. The unanalysed basis of this orientation is made clear when I point it out to colleagues and they reply 'Yes, of course that's what we aim to do', and no alternatives are imagined possible.

Now I do not conclude that there is a prevalent feature of the 'personalities' of these teachers which explains the focus on evaluation, and on the observable performance aspects of their colleagues. Rather I have come to recognise a very strong set of forces in the environment which play a large part in creating this picture. Let me mention three. First, the dominant discourse in our education system currently is one emphasising performance. The advent of 'performance tables' for schools, a focus on pupils' test and exam performance, and talk of 'performance management' for teachers, all play their part. The discourse of 'standards' and the addition of mechanical approaches to target-setting – both for teachers and for pupils – add to the picture. Second, the act of classroom observation can unwittingly engender an orientation which focuses on the teacher rather than the whole event and on assumed deficits rather than the complex detail of interaction and learning. For example, when teachers observe a video of a classroom: if given no structure for their observations and no guidance for their role, observers tend to focus on the teacher and focus on the negative. In doing so they adopt the role of hostile witness which is all too prevalent in the public discourse on the inspection of schools. Third, life in classrooms is full of evaluation: a public evaluation of someone or someone's performance is made in a classroom every couple of minutes (Doyle 1980). The effect of this on teachers' perspective is considerable in my view: they tend to react with suspicion to the addition of further evaluative schemes, as is evidenced in reactions to teacher appraisal, and they do not accept the views of policy-makers which seem to imply that the purposes of education are encapsulated in what may be assessed.

I am convinced that these environmental and situational forces explain the performance evaluation orientation because of the variations I see, both within and beyond teacher mentoring. It appears most in initial teacher education where 'standards' and competences dominate much of the school-based agenda, and teachers assess beginners. Until recently it has been a little less intense in the mentoring of newly qualified teachers, and, of the teacher contexts, it is at its least in headteacher mentoring, where the main theme is handling multiple pressures while still leading a learning community. This orientation is not present in other mentoring contexts I have experienced, for example a mentoring scheme for black and ethnic minority employees in the BBC (Watkins 1997b). In that setting 'feedback' is rarely mentioned and is not problematic – the idea that the mentor is to judge the mentee's performance simply does not arise. Instead, and with little guidance, the mentor–mentee pairs get on with constructing a highly engaged programme of activity, exchange and discussion to promote learning. It's a hard job at the best of times to help another person learn, and the contextual pressures on teachers do not make it any easier.

WHAT'S WRONG WITH PERFORMANCE ORIENTATION?

Lest anyone be in doubt, or those who have adopted the mechanical discourse try to read me otherwise, I seek the highest quality in teachers and expect to see this reflected, in part, in the way they are in classrooms. What is at issue is how high levels of performance should be achieved, and this soon relates to the issue of how high levels of performance are conceptualised. The problem with a performance stance is that:

- it does not promote optimum processes and levels of learning;
- it may mis-represent what is most important in teaching;
- it may damage learning relationships between teachers;
- it may lead to lower standards in the school system.

The difference between performance orientation and learning orientation has been researched since the ground-breaking work of Carol Dweck (see, for example, Dweck 1986; Dweck and Leggett 1988; Smiley and Dweck 1994). Learners with a performance orientation persist less, have more negative views about their abilities and display helplessness when the task is difficult. By contrast, those with a learning orientation show greater persistence, have flexible views of themselves, and are more likely to work effectively in solving difficult problems. So to emphasise performance rather than learning as a goal can be counter-productive.

The performance idea that the important things about teaching are the observables does not fit with current understandings of pedagogy which highlight the complexity of orchestrating the classroom context, the multiple nature of teacher knowledge and the connected nature of teacher understanding (Watkins and Mortimore 1999). It may also blind us from other avenues through which teachers learn, including reflecting on their conception of teaching (Freeman 1991) and hearing narratives of other learners who have made the transformation to teaching (James 1997).

If teachers behave towards each other like hostile witnesses, this may put at risk the trust which is necessary for building a sense of professional community in a school, a major feature of it as a learning community (Kruse *et al.* 1995).

In the current context where schools are judged by performance measures, the most recent evidence (Gray *et al.* 1999) shows that the most improving schools maintain an overarching focus on learning. Given that the knowledge base in society is expanding and changing rapidly, and skills of learning about learning are recognised as important for pupils, a focus on teaching as performance seems increasingly anachronistic, and unlikely to elicit the most from the school system. As Doyle puts it: '[the use of] generic indicators of effectiveness and isolated classroom practices . . . will inevitably narrow and distort the purposes and achievements of schools' (Doyle 1990: 354).

PERFORMANCE FEEDBACK: COMMON PRACTICES AND THEIR IMPACT

Discussions between teachers following a shared experience of a classroom are often handled with a very high focus on judgement of personal performance: in the case of conversations between beginner teachers and their mentors it can constitute up to 60 per cent of the exchange (Haggarty 1995a). Yet nearly a century ago Dewey highlighted the dangers:

> It ought to go without saying (unfortunately it does not in all cases) that criticism should be directed to making the professional student thoughtful about his work in the light of principles, rather than to induce in him a recognition that certain special methods are good and certain other special methods bad. At all events, *no greater travesty of intellectual criticism* can be given than to set a student to teaching a brief number of lessons, have him under inspection in practically all the time of every lesson, and then criticise him, almost if not quite, at the very end of each lesson, upon the particular way in which that particular lesson has been taught, pointing out elements of failure and success. Such methods of criticism . . . are not calculated to develop a thoughtful and independent teacher.
>
> (Dewey 1904)

The focus on judgement is reflected in rather than challenged by much of the 'practical' advice which is given to mentors and appraisers.

The advice 'Start with the positive' has been widespread, so much so that it has influenced roles and expectations in a subtle but widespread fashion. Many teachers who are receiving feedback now expect it in this form, and are sitting quietly waiting for the negative to arrive. I have even experienced secondary school students remarking on a progress report from a teacher: 'Ah, but he's starting with the positive'. More recently a new variant of this advice has arisen: the 'feedback sandwich' – positive, negative, positive. Attempts to disguise the judgement of 'good and bad' by the common language of 'strengths and weaknesses' does not cover up the basic stance of judgement. A clear recognition of this comes from an eleven-year-old boy: 'They talk about strengths and weaknesses but strengths are always the things we need to get more of and weaknesses are what we've already got' (Perry 1999: 65).

Such 'positive and negative' communication is not integrated by the receiver, but organised into separate categories in a process of compartmentalisation (Showers 1992). We subsequently activate positive self-aspects, and minimise access to negative information. It promotes defensiveness on the part of the 'receiver'. Many beginner teachers learn how to 'play the game' of evaluative relations with their mentors. Disagreements or extended discussions of the performance judgements are not a common part of the conversation: rather an atmosphere of politeness descends, and both parties work to get the event completed with minimum difficulty.

So instead of seeking and welcoming feedback as a source of interest and learning, feedback for many teachers becomes something which you didn't necessarily ask for, but which punctuates your life and learning in ways for which you find methods of coping. Systems of appraisal can become ceremonial and perfunctory (Frase 1992), with little or no impact on improving teaching and learning, only complied with to meet policy requirements. Such schemes are looked upon with suspicion by many classroom teachers. Streshly (1992) suggests that teachers view performance through standardised testing with anxiety and resentment, because the results threaten to judge incorrectly their efforts, and the fact that some managers regard testing as another means of teacher surveillance only reduces the value of the feedback to teachers. Surveillance does not provide the conditions for teachers to take active responsibility for their learning.

Defensiveness may also emerge for the mentor, as shown in a limited focus (Edwards and Collison 1995), and the fact that they talk a lot. As one researcher concludes: 'many mentors talk about their own generalised theories of teaching, with little reference to the realities of practice. Listening to students and addressing their learning seems to take place only occasionally, if at all' (Haggarty 1995b: 41). Similarly, Zeichner and Liston (1985) found little focus in post-observation discussions on what students were trying to accomplish – their reasons and goals. Which is all the more frustrating given the comment: 'Almost any kind of feedback can be enjoyable provided it is logically related to a goal in which one has invested psychic energy' (Csikszentmihalyi 1990: 57). Even in headteacher mentoring, a focus on clarifying and realising goals may be missing: Southworth's (1995) review concludes that although there is the potential for stimulating critical, reflective, learner-oriented leadership, the reality may be more one of passing on conservative role assumptions.

The responsibilities of the two parties can become distorted. The person giving feedback appears to take on a responsibility for the other person's development, especially if they also start to set targets for the other person to achieve, and the receiver in turn does not engage her/his responsibility in that process.

To avoid the negative impacts outlined above, current practice can be extended by extending the focus, goals and conception of feedback. I find that teachers engage with such extensions readily: they affirm them as learning professionals in a way which takes them out of the rut of the dominant assumptions.

EXTENSION ONE: THE FOCUS OF FEEDBACK

A first step towards improvement may be to extend the focus of feedback wider than the performance judgement in current practices. In the list below I propose nine different types of feedback, each of which has a different focus: an attempt has been made to offer an indicative example as though the feedback agent was another teacher.

- *Data feedback* – aspects of performance
  Example: 'you used twelve closed questions and three open ones'
- *Contextual feedback* – data on features of the social or educational context
  Example: 'these pupils have a negative reputation in the school'; 'they haven't been taught about fractions yet'
- *Information feedback* – data which have been selected and interpreted to inform
  Example: 'when you gave the class a collaborative group task they seemed to be more engaged'

- *Knowledge feedback* – what has been learnt, what meaning created
  Example: 'your second explanation of floating made new sense for me and for some of the pupils I think'
- *Vision feedback* – how participants perceive the purposes and goals
  Example: 'your description of doing mathematics was inspiring'
- *Process feedback* – how the social and interpersonal processes operate
  Example: 'it seemed that the task didn't really reward collaboration, since dominant leaders emerged in the groups'
- *Improvement feedback* – what would make a difference
  Example: 'some of the class suggested that they needed more time on the second activity'
- *Change feedback* – how innovations are being received
  Example: 'I had the impression that they enjoyed the new challenge of text analysis'
- *Learning feedback* – metacognitions which have been stimulated
  Example: 'while watching this class I wondered about the depth of ideas in one I teach'

All nine types are examples of feedback as it is commonly understood: one person making comments to another person on aspects of a shared experience which s/he, the reporter, has selected. Nothing has yet been said about whether, or under what conditions, any of this process may support learning. Perhaps the later types in this list suggest a different way of handling feedback that could lead to a different type of learning, but the notion of teacher feedback in relation to learning remains unquestioned.

However, my experience of seeing teachers experiment with some of these suggests that they find themselves involved in different types of conversation from those they had previously experienced, conversations with more depth and range. In this way they see more possibilities in a post-observation discussion, especially how most constructive feedback is free from evaluation (Kilbourn 1990). This is linked with broadening the focus beyond the person and can have significant effects. Kamins and Dweck (1999) have shown that when feedback is focused on the process rather than the person, whether it is criticism or praise, recipients subsequently display significantly less 'helpless' responses (including self-blame). So person feedback even when positive, can create vulnerability and a sense of only being worthy under certain conditions: this undermines subsequent coping.

The trend which is roughly implied in the above nine, also leads to another step which is to ensure that feedback for learning lives up to its name and has an explicit focus on learning.

EXTENSION TWO: FEEDBACK FOR LEARNING

Teachers generally recognise that a focus on learning can enhance performance, whereas a focus on performance can depress performance: when they do so, they enable themselves to create much more generative exchanges. To promote feedback for learning, an explicit view on learning is needed. A simple model which highlights some of the steps in learning from experience is given in Figure 5.1a.

This model on its own can increase focus on the learner teacher's learning, and its various stages. It can sometimes highlight difficulties which a learner teacher experiences at one stage or another. It indicates that feedback must be sought, that a stock of strategies is needed for reviewing, and that choosing new action for the next cycle is a key element.

The model can also be developed to plan activities which promote action-reflection learning by the learner (Watkins and Whalley 1993). Such activities may be observations, investigations, or personal actions: they need to cover all four stages for the learning cycle to be complete (Figure 5.1b). This model can act as a useful framework for a learning discussion, following planned or unplanned activities, especially if plainly in view for all parties.

It now becomes possible to specify what someone whose aim is to offer feedback might best do in order to promote the cycle of action learning. At each stage of Figure 5.1c, what they offer parallels the stages of the learner's cycle.

While working on this framework with teachers, I have found the following:

- Starting with commentary helps to avoid starting with judgement. It affirms that the valuable extra contribution which is brought is observation, an extra set of eyes. A conversation which starts in this way is often appropriately focused on more than just the learner teacher.
- Moving to identify issues becomes less fraught for all concerned after some commentary has been offered, partly because it is likely that a real dialogue will have started, and the learner her/himself will be identifying issues from her/his perspective.
- The stage of offering analysis requires the person offering feedback

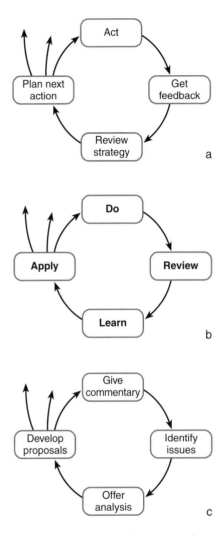

Figure 5.1 Elements in learning cycles and feedback cycles: (a) learning from experience; (b) planned learning activities; (c) feedback for learning

to be explicit on the view of classrooms which they hold such that they have identified the particular issues as important. It also reduces the risk of them taking too much time on generalised theories of teaching, with little reference to the detail.

- The idea of developing proposals together is not radical, but if it is done after a good analysis the learner teacher will be able to see, at best, how a colleague chooses practical actions to realise their image of a classroom.

The ordering of the four stages is important: teachers may already have available elements of all four, but structuring them in the framework seems to help them order their contribution to the conversation. Operation of this model also seems to help them clarify their own voice in a way which does not depend on making judgements. It takes the pressure off their construction of their role and reduces the anxiety which may previously have characterised their contribution.

I do not offer the framework in Figure 5.1c with the idea that one teacher extols his/her opinions in each stage and leaves the receiver to make of it what they will. The quality of interchange at each stage is crucial, and dialogic conversation is what is most likely to support lasting learning. That point requires us to recognise the view of learning on which it is based.

EXTENSION THREE: THE UNDERLYING VIEW OF LEARNING AND FEEDBACK

The third extension depends on unearthing and extending the views of learning which inform our approach to feedback. Bruner (1996) identifies four views of learning which have held sway in our times. Simply put, these are:

1   learning by being shown;
2   learning by being told;
3   learning by constructing meaning; and
4   learning by being part of a knowledge-generating community.

Each has an associated conception of feedback – except the first, a very simple model with the implied notion of imitation, which does not explain much and under-estimates a great deal about complex human processes.

Learning by being told is a dominant view: it relates to the idea of teaching as instruction, and in this view feedback is the correction of performance. This stems from a mechanical metaphor, in which the oft-quoted example is a thermostat: a sensor picks up information from the environment, and if the temperature is above a set level, the heating is shut off; if the temperature falls below another level the heating is turned on again. This is a 'closed' system: it operates independently from other systems, and the range of options is limited: feedback reduces deviation from a norm, and maintains a status quo. Sometimes we think that this model of feedback describes human behaviour, such as learning a motor skill through self-corrective feedback. For example, when learning to steer a car, the driver learns how much to move the steering wheel, receives immediate visual information about the result of the action and can make corrections accordingly. In time the steering becomes smooth and accurate. However, this is a simple and idealised description of a closed system, and real-life steering is more complex. Other aspects arise – the sudden appearance of an oncoming car, an icy morning, whether the driver had breakfast, the driver's self-beliefs – and affect the real situation so that the performance may break down, showing the idealised view to be inadequate. The complexity of human motor performance has required that the notion of 'feed forward' be invented: people not only learn from the results of their actions, they also anticipate actions which have never yet occurred.

Attempts have been made to address social performance by analogy with motor skills. The social skills model (Argyle 1967: 70 – see Figure 5.2) gives a key role to feedback, but it soon becomes clear that this is not a simple process of 'correction'.

Each element of this model is highly complex: for example, the element 'translation' encapsulates the active 'reading' of the social world, the understanding of the social world, one's options in it and one's prediction about others' behaviour. Still the model does not represent real-life, real-time social interaction. It reminds us that feedback, like all other human communication, is always interpreted and its impact is subject to the person's goals and 'translation' processes. In addition, the

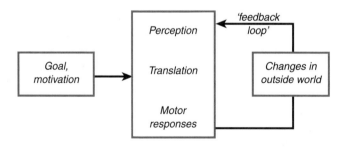

Figure 5.2 Model of social skills

simple assumption that someone who is 'giving feedback' is a credible source may not be valid, especially since mentors in many schemes are allocated rather than chosen. The assumption remains that feedback 'given' is a major source of learning. Such a view can under-estimate the extent to which teachers learn from a range of sources (Smylie 1989) including their pupils (Meyer 1995). It can also down-play the significance of human beings being self-defining (Ford 1987). From this perspective, self-reflection is a more frequent and more crucial determinant of self-knowledge than social mechanisms including feedback (see, for example, Sedikides and Skowronski 1995).

The stability assumed by the closed system view may not obtain, as shown in those interactions which escalate. For example, if teachers read each other as threatening, their next response may be to increase demand or increase intransigence according to their goal or motivation. In work on families as complex systems, early ideas of feedback saw it as maintaining the homeostasis of the family. This view has been abandoned, as a partial view with mechanical assumptions (Hoffman 1993: 82). The contemporary shift in thinking has been to communication and conversation metaphors: in these, inter-subjective loops of dialogue may represent what we took feedback to represent. Thus we need to cast the notion of feedback into a communications concept, and focus on communicative processes between teachers.

This moves us to consider Bruner's third view of learning – the construction of meaning – reflecting recent research. The processes whereby one person supports another in constructing meaning are complex: the focus requires an important switch to the learner and their learning. One principle is to draw out their current conceptions and add variation to them, through reviewing experience with an explicit focus on meaning-making. Thus learners are supported in explaining to themselves the experiences they meet, and Chi *et al.* (1994) demonstrate that this improves understanding. Accumulated evidence about learning (Marton and Booth 1997) suggests it is more accurate to view learning as adding additional perspectives to our current meanings, rather than replacing the 'incorrect'. Indeed 'misconceptions' can have considerable longevity in the face of refuting evidence.

If we view teachers as complex makers of meaning, a different view of teacher competences is required from that which circulates currently. We need a view of the professional as having goals, being involved in their own learning, and having competences for learning about learning. Figure 5.3 sketches competences which are important for high-level teaching and learning. Higher levels imply greater complexity and reflexivity: they may be founded on having some/many of the lower level competences in the repertoire. Upward movement through the levels is stimulated by the sort of learning which expands possibilities, helps the learner add extra variations to their repertoire, and helps them integrate these into a meta-perspective.

A meta-perspective highlights the important influence of context on learning, so that the view of learning as construction soon embraces the fact that for teachers this is taking place in a school. This was the fourth view identified by Bruner (1996): learning by being part of a knowledge-generating community. Sadly, many teachers say that their schools would not be well described in these terms. Nevertheless, schools with a collaborative approach to teacher relations promote ongoing learning and development for teachers, and for pupils, 'We also find that the greater teachers' opportunities for learning, the more their students tend to learn' (Rosenholtz 1991: 7). Here 'feedback' takes on a much more multiple view, and highlights the qualities of the context, where many parties interact and continuously produce and receive feedback. Learning is fostered through co-construction, exchanging narratives in the process we call dialogue, which again includes self-explanation (Chi 1996). It does not make for a uniform product, nor is it limited to officially sanctioned relations such as mentoring. Hawkey (1995a, b) found that peer work was of primary importance in the development of beginner teachers' meta-learning, the process of understanding their own teaching style. They rarely offered each other advice or questioned each other but rather engaged in

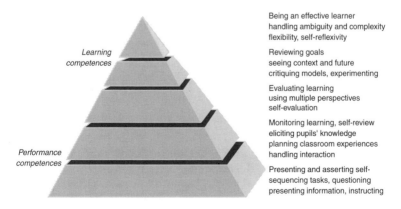

Figure 5.3 A model of teacher competences

parallel, rather disconnected conversations that gave an opportunity for each to clarify and develop their own thoughts about their own teaching. So in a learning-centred community of this sort, one would expect to find:

- an explicit focus on learning, and an explicit model of learning (such as Figure 5.1b);
- practices such as learners generating their own questions;
- learners being asked to make sense (to themselves and to others) of what they meet;
- promotion of dialogue and collaboration;
- reviews of the *learning*, as opposed to performance; and
- a building-up of narrative about learning.

In this fourth model, the focus shifts to the processes of building a community of learners engaged in the generation and evaluation of knowledge. Teachers work with colleagues as 'sounding boards' and co-investigators, and find their own voice (Featherstone *et al.* 1997) Dialogue is supported through structures and cultures, and lies at the heart of learning which is both widespread and deep.

In my own practice as an educator, I have recently experienced situations which parallel those discussed in this chapter, *viz.* peer observation of teaching and appraisal. In both cases the situations have been handled with a primary focus on learning rather than performance, and in a group climate which aims to value exchange. They have each led to very rich dialogue and to the co-construction of high-level personal learning insights. I am confident that they have also contributed to the co-construction of my own enhanced performance.

REFERENCES

Argyle, M. (1967) *The Psychology of Interpersonal Behaviour*, London: Penguin.

Bruner, J. S. (1996) *The Culture of Education*, Cambridge MA: Harvard University Press.

Chi, M. T. H. (1996) 'Constructing self-explanations and scaffolded explanations in tutoring', *Applied Cognitive Psychology* 10: Special Issue, S33–S49.

Chi, M. T. H., de Leeuw, N., Chiu, M.-H. and LaVancher, C. (1994) 'Eliciting self-explanations improves understanding', *Cognitive Science* 18, 439–477.

Csikszentmihalyi, M. (1990) *Flow: the psychology of optimal experience*, New York: Harper and Row.

Dewey, J. (1904) 'The relation of theory to practice in education', in C. McMurray (ed.) *The Third Yearbook of the National Society for the Scientific Study of Education, Part 1,* Chicago: University of Chicago Press.

Doyle, W. (1980) *Classroom Management,* West Lafayette IN: Kappa Delta Pi.

Doyle, W. (1990) 'Classroom knowledge as a foundation for teaching', *Teachers College Record* 91:3, 347–360.

Dweck, C. (1986) 'Motivational processes affecting learning', *American Psychologist* 41:10, 1040–1048.

Dweck, C. and Leggett, E. L. (1988) 'A social-cognitive approach to motivation and personality', *Psychological Review* 95:2, 256–273.

Edwards, A. and Collison, J. (1995) *Mentoring and Developing Practice in Primary Schools: supporting student teacher learning in schools,* Buckingham: Open University Press.

Featherstone, D., Munby, H. and Russell, T. (1997) *Finding a Voice while Learning to Teach: others' voices can help you find your own,* London: Falmer.

Ford, D. H. (1987) *Humans as Self-Constructing Living Systems: a developmental perspective on behavior and personality,* Hillsdale, NJ: Lawrence Erlbaum.

Frase, L. E. (1992) 'Constructive feedback on teaching is missing', *Education* 113:2, 176–181.

Freeman, D. (1991) '"To make the tacit explicit": teacher education, emerging discourse, and conceptions of teaching', *Teaching and Teacher Education* 7:5–6, 439–454.

Gray, J., Hopkins, D., Reynolds, D., Wilcox, B., Farrell, S. and Jesson, D. (1999) *Improving Schools: performance and potential,* Buckingham: Open University Press.

Haggarty, L. (1995a) 'The use of content analysis to explore conversations between school teacher mentors and student teachers', *British Educational Research Journal* 21:2, 183–197.

Haggarty, L. (1995b) 'The complexities of effective mentoring in initial teacher education', *Mentoring and Tutoring* 2:3, 32–41.

Hawkey, K. (1995a) 'Peer support and the development of metalearning in school-based initial teacher education', unpublished paper presented at Annual Meeting of the American Educational Research Association, San Francisco.

Hawkey, K. (1995b) 'Learning from peers: the experience of student teachers in school-based teacher education', *Journal of Teacher Education* 46: 3, 175–183.

Hoffman, L. (1993) *Exchanging Voices: a collaborative approach to family therapy,* London: Karnac Books.

James, P. (1997) 'Transformative learning: promoting change across cultural worlds', *Journal of Vocational Education and Training: The Vocational Aspect of Education* 49:2, 197–219.

Kamins, M. L. and Dweck, C. S. (1999) 'Person versus process praise and criticism: implications for contingent self-worth and coping', *Developmental Psychology* 35:3, 835–847.

Kilbourn, B. (1990) *Constructive Feedback: learning the art*, Toronto: Ontario Institute for Studies in Education.

Kruse, S. D., Louis, K. S. and Bryk, A. S. (1995) 'An emerging framework for analyzing school-based professional community', in K. S. Louis, S. D. Kruse and Associates (eds) *Professionalism and Community: perspectives on reforming urban schools*, Thousand Oaks CA: Corwin.

Marton, F. and Booth, S. (1997) *Learning and Awareness*, Mahwah, NJ: Lawrence Erlbaum.

Meyer, R. J. (1995) 'Stories to teach and teaching to story: the use of narrative in learning to teach', *Language Arts* 72:4, 276–278.

Perry, L. (1999) 'There's a garden – somewhere', in A. Morgan (ed.) *Once Upon a Time: narrative therapy with children and their families*, Adelaide: Dulwich Centre Publications.

Rosenholtz, S. J. (1991) *Teachers' Workplace: the social organization of schools*, New York: Teachers College Press.

Sedikides, C. and Skowronski, J. (1995) 'On the sources of self-knowledge – the perceived primacy of self-reflection', *Journal of Social and Clinical Psychology* 14:3, 244–270.

Showers, C. (1992) 'Compartmentalization of positive and negative self-knowledge – keeping bad apples out of the bunch', *Journal of Personality and Social Psychology* 62:6, 1036–1049.

Smiley, P. A. and Dweck, C. S. (1994) 'Individual differences in achievement goals among young children', *Child Development* 65:6, 1723–1743.

Smylie, M. (1989) 'Teachers' views of the effectiveness of sources of learning to teach', *Elementary School Journal* 89:5, 543–558.

Southworth, G. (1995) 'Reflections on mentoring for new school leaders', *Journal of Educational Administration*. 33:5, 17–28.

Streshly, W.A. (1992) 'The feedback loop', *Education* 113:2, 182–186.

Watkins, C. (1992) 'An experiment in mentor training', in M. Wilkin (ed.) *Mentoring in Schools*, London: Kogan Page.

Watkins, C. (1997a) 'Clarifying mentoring goals in their context', in J. Stephenson (ed.) *Mentoring – the New Panacea?*, Dereham: Peter Francis.

Watkins, C. (1997b) *Mentoring Scheme for Black and Ethnic Minority Staff: Evaluation Report at the end of one year of the scheme*, London: Institute of Education/BBC.

Watkins, C. and Mortimore, P. (1999) 'Pedagogy: what do we know?', in P. Mortimore (ed.) *Pedagogy and its Impact on Learning*, London: Paul Chapman/Sage.

Watkins, C. and Whalley, C. (1993) *Mentoring: resources for school-based development*, Harlow: Longman.

Watkins, C. and Whalley, C. (1995) 'Mentoring beginner teachers – issues for schools to anticipate and manage', in T. Kerry and A. S. Mayes (eds) *Issues in Mentoring*, London: Routledge and Open University.

Zeichner, K. M. and Liston, D. P. (1985) 'Varieties of discourse in supervisory conferences', *Teaching and Teacher Education* 1:2, 155–174.

6 Student views on careers education and guidance – what sort of feedback to careers co-ordinators?

Jacqui MacDonald

INTRODUCTION

The comments of young people on careers work in schools are seldom asked for and therefore seldom given. This chapter describes a study based on interviews with over 150 young people to explore their views on the quality and content of careers education and guidance. In the context of various stated aims for careers education, the views of young people are reported. The lack of impact, the wish for real challenge, and issues of inequality and exclusion are raised. Evidence of good communication between students and teachers over such issues seems to be lacking. I argue that the only way in which careers education can support all students is by asking them, through feedback, what they think about current practice and how they see their needs and experiences.

CAREERS EDUCATION AND GUIDANCE – THE OFFICIAL VIEW

Careers education and guidance is broadly defined as a range of processes designed to enable individuals to make informed choices and transitions related to their learning and to their work. It is seen as providing opportunities for young people to acquire the skills, knowledge and understanding necessary to enable them to manage their career or path through life. 'A career path might include a range of stages including formal jobs at different organisations, freelance work, training and re-training, formal education, voluntary work, caring work at home and perhaps periods of unemployment' (Hoffbrand *et al.* 1998: 2/1).

Legislation of the last decade continues the claim that careers education and guidance has 'an important contribution to make to the work of schools in preparing pupils for the opportunities, responsibilities and experiences of adult life' (Education Reform Act 1988, Section one). The implication is that students will be made employable through a career programme, that schooling will not be viewed just as the place to gain qualifications, but a forum for the acquisition and development of a range of skills.

More recently, DfEE (1994) has proposed ten principles for good quality careers education and guidance in schools. Subsequent Government documents have continued the image of 'Better Choices' as the goal of careers education. Government White Papers on the theme of 'Competitiveness' (e.g. DTI 1994) have used the image of global markets to raise the expectations of careers education and guidance, and of co-operation between schools and careers services. Careers education and guidance and at least one week's work experience are now an entitlement of all young people. A further dimension was added by an education White Paper (DfEE 1997) which referred to the importance of effective partnerships between education and business, and the need for lifelong learning. Thus Government thinking is placed within an economic context and has moved careers beyond the realm of schools acting alone, into an area of work that appeared to need the involvement of other sectors of society in different ways.

The current importance of careers work in schools and colleges is deemed to relate to the changing nature of the world of work, which in turn is linked to changes in the economy, new technology and future patterns of work. The idea of a job for life is seen as a thing of the past, so that learning for lifelong career development becomes a priority rather than the simple making of choices on leaving school. A long-standing model of decision making, opportunity awareness, transition skills and self-awareness, 'DOTS', is now being supplanted by a model of the development of career management skills. Thus SCAA (1996) argued that 'Continuing changes in the pattern and nature of education, training and work require pupils to develop skills which will enable them to take greater responsibility for managing their lifelong learning and career development' (page 1). The skills were described as:

Decision-making: How will I choose effectively between my options?
Action planning: How will I set and reach my goals?
Negotiating: How will I reach the agreements needed to implement my decisions?

Self-presentation: How will I present myself to make the most of the opportunities I secure?

The emphasis on career management skills is based on the belief that this would 'foster self reliance, autonomy and flexibility, enabling people to manage their own career development within and outside of organisations' (SCAA 1996: 1).

In the view of Government and its agencies, a rising profile of careers work is to equip young people with the skills necessary to be useful employees. Whether teachers have the guidance and resources to implement this, and whether pupils experience it this way remains an open question.

RESEARCH CONTEXT

This chapter is based on a research project which I carried out between July 1996 and July 1998, which aimed to explore what was happening in schools following the range of developments which were taking place at that time in the field of careers education and guidance. Schools were awash with moneys for a variety of initiatives; documents based on this area of work were being published at regular and short intervals. This was clearly supposedly a glorious time for careers; it was flavour of the month and had moved from being what one can only describe from a Cinderella position to the saviour of the economy.

The plan for this research was to explore what careers co-ordinators and advisers thought about current careers practice, how heads of years viewed their role and responsibilities, what head teachers felt about careers and what students had to say about careers practice.

A mixed methodology was employed, using questionnaires to a small sample, and semi-structured interviews with individual students, teachers and small groups of students. Student respondents numbered 150 from five co-educational schools in the London region. Years 9 to 13 were represented, 80 female and 70 male. Ethnic categories were: White 58, Black (African, African Caribbean) 65, Asian 15, Mixed race 12. All interviews with students (and those with the various staff) were recorded and transcribed,

From the number of themes which emerged from this research, the most significant was what students had to say about careers work in schools. The interviews seem to have been very successful in capturing their experiences and opinions about careers education and guidance.

On reflection this success may reflect the role of the external researcher, as a somewhat detached third party. Students felt able to talk openly about their experiences of careers lessons. Perhaps they recognised that it was not my practice that they were challenging; and that I would not take their comments as a personal affront. Potential difficulties in replicating such a process between the same students and their teachers were already being indicated.

CAREERS EDUCATION AND GUIDANCE – STUDENTS' VIEWS

In this account I select four aspects of their programmes on which the young people commented – goals, status, divisions and quality of learning – before building an analysis in terms of teacher–pupil relationships.

Goals

The central purpose of programmes and activities was not of high value for many:

> I think we could make better use of our time. (year 11)

> un-important, irrelevant . . . a waste of time. (year 12)

> Even on reflection, I don't really see what I gained from it. (year 13)

> all the [careers] lessons we've had have been quite hopeless. A lot of people just didn't get anything out of it I don't think . . . most of my friends and I in particular; couldn't really see the point. (year 13)

Students indicated a basic agreement with what they thought the purpose could or should be.

> We're getting to an age now where we need to make up our minds. This is the most important subject for us at the moment. (year 11 students)

> When I think about the lessons, the ideas behind it was quite good, but . . . I think it makes you think or at least try to make you think in a different way, and to look at yourself and make you study how you work and things like that. (year 11)

Other comments were about helping them to find a job, finding out where they could study, a particular course. Careers was seen as an information giving service. None spoke about it in terms of the transferable skills they could develop, to help them to identify their strengths or how through a range of activities and real experiences they could better manage their progression in their learning and work as they move through school and beyond.

The young people interviewed appeared to be arguing that a better shared vision would lead to greater enthusiasm for the area.

> you need a programme that the teacher understands and believes in, and that we understand and believe in. So students feel that what they're going to get at the end will help them in some way. (year 13)

The notion of careers work providing a challenge to their thinking, knowledge and understanding. The opportunity to apply abstract knowledge to real experiences was welcome by them but their experience of lessons did not match this goal.

Status of the provision

Careers provision often seen to be 'tacked' on at the end of the day and is not taken seriously in terms of timetabling.

> Ours [careers lesson] is at the end of the day and when we get there, everyone's just knackered. (year 10)

Amount of time was also being squeezed. Many schools felt forced to prioritise time on the timetable on the basis of expediency and league tables. The careers programme is often down-graded and in some instances disappearing altogether. This seems to show that schools do not see it as important.

> lessons are too short . . . by the time we get there from our other lessons you have about 20 minutes then you have to pack up. (year 11)

Some students felt that there was little status afforded by some of their teachers:

> I mean having a teacher saying 'well I don't know why I do it, I

was just given it, and I'm handing it to you' just gives you no confidence that what you're doing is of any worth at all. (year 13)

We got on really well with our tutor and I think she saw it along the same lines as us . . . just saw it as pointless. (year 12)

Divisions and distance

Students raised issues of inequality and exclusion. For example, several students felt a sense of unfairness in terms of how placements were allocated.

I didn't go to a placement of [my] choice, it was a waste of time. By the time the list got to our class, there was nothing left. (year 10)

Others felt that teachers were prepared to go out of their way to meet their requirements:

My Head of Year organised my work experience with his neighbour who works for a large Graphic design company. The company wasn't really looking for anyone. They really took me as a favour. (year 11)

And for others the opportunities made available through family and friends indicated the different cultural capital available to some (a fact which young people themselves acknowledged):

My father's an editor of commercials and pop videos and he arranged for me to go to one of his clients. It was a lot of fun, lots of free lunches, free tickets.

Work experience was organised through my uncle who lives in France with an Opera company. (year 12)

My father has introduced me to a lot of different films, books and photography, to different people and different kinds of music (year 13)

The potential learning resource of the community, beyond the teacher's grasp and unequally distributed, was nevertheless clear. Issues of social class clearly influenced students' thoughts about work opportunities and their perceptions about their capabilities, but did not seem to be addressed in the programmes.

The people I mix with although I don't think I'm purposely kind of elitist or anything, a lot of the people that I have around me have been the ones that have applied to Oxbridge. (year 13)

I think it's easy for someone like me – you know, middle class, with support at home. (year 13)

For some, what learnings of a 'life-long' nature that were reported seemed to emanate from particular family experiences. Those who saw parents as continually stressed, feeling the need to work until they retired, took the message.

I don't want to be doing the same job until I collect my pension. It seems really scary that the only time you can probably live is when you're old. (year 12)

Several students felt their needs were neglected in selection of placements and felt alienated by the experience. A black student described an experience which he felt unable to cope with on his own and even though he mentioned it to the teacher who carried out the placement visit, no action was taken by the school and the student received no debriefing as to how he could have dealt with the situation

I was working for a plumbing and heating company and was put with a man called R and we went out to a job up London. We had different jobs and for the whole day I sat in the van for one of the jobs. They weren't going to let me into this house, because it was an old lady's house. The other jobs, I sat either on the stairway or on a chair nearby, being on my own; listening to my Walkman.

When asked to explain why he thought he was treated in this way, he said:

Because they was like thinking . . . that I was going to take money, attack her or something . . . they didn't say it exactly. I don't know why. They shouldn't take me on if that's how they were going to think of me. (year 10)

In this case neither the preparation for work experience nor the general careers programme addressed issues of inequality in terms of race and gender or other forms of discrimination. There were some indications that the negative experiences that students are exposed to in the outside world were avoided. This is reflected in a conversation with a group of young men:

M. Teachers don't spend much time with you as they do with other students. You have to try to motivate yourself a bit more.
R. Yeah, some teachers work on the stereotype that you must be this way or that way. That you must want to do this or that . . . because . . . you know.
M. And they don't even know anything about you.
R. You get inspired by different things. Seeing my Mum having to work so hard and my Dad like telling me that I have to work hard, I need to be better than the next man.
X. Sometimes you're made to feel that it's not right for you to think that you want to do such and such . . . but why not? (year 12)

Their life experiences play a vital role in how students view their school experiences. It is therefore misleading to treat students as a homogeneous group, particularly when one considers the diversity that makes up the student population.

Quality of learning

Learning, when it was mentioned, seemed to be incidental to the programme in the eyes of the students. Many times students chose to report whether they enjoyed something rather than whether they had learnt.

I enjoyed it [work experience] but I didn't see what it had to do with school. I was working in a food type place. I was making pizzas, cutting them. But the only thing that it had to do with school was my reading and that isn't very good, but I still got along, so reading wasn't important anyway. (year 10)

I was too tired most days to really enjoy it [work experience] (year 10)

For another group, while they had learnt from their work experience, the idea that their career lessons had facilitated such learning was notably absent.

Work experience reminded me why I was at school . . . to get qualifications, to be able to do a job properly. (year 10)

I'm not exactly the same person. But that's part of working really, everyone has to put on that little . . . it's not so much an act, it's just like knowing how to talk to certain people . . . it's about being two different people . . . because I can do it, I can dress properly and talk to people. It's not what a lot of people expect from us [black student] but I can do it, be as good as anyone else. (year 11)

We had a lot of preparation and that was very useful, that was one of the main things that teach you about the outside. (year 11)

For one group of students their major memories of careers lessons were the procedural elements, to which they developed a strategic response:

I. What do you remember most?
R. Apart from work experience?
H. Thousands and thousands of action plans!
C. Oh, I know by heart what to put in them, I know exactly what they want to hear, and I know exactly what phrases to use!
R. We had to write another one this week as well, which is so tedious. (year 12)

The procedural blanket nature of the provision stimulated ideas for improvement.

I think you need a few careers lessons but then you should be able to say, I don't want any more for now. (year 13)

And an investigative approach to career learning was proposed:

I would have liked more time for work experience, and I would have liked to have been given a set of objectives. I would have liked to have been given or been asked to think of 10 or 20 questions to do with life, working life and been asked to ask members of the workforce 'How do you cope with . . . ?, What do you think about the status of you in this job . . . ?, What scope is there for you to develop in this job?'. (year 13)

Student comments indicate a need for programmes where students can learn from each other, but there was little mention of active or collaborative learning. From this evidence, the orientation of careers work tends to be counter-productive. Activities appear to be teacher-driven rather than an opportunity for independent thinking and learning. Thus lessons provide little challenge or development. The hurried nature of the provision seemed to lead to a disparate programme. Rudduck reminds us that 'what students have to say about teaching and learning is not only worth listening to but provides an important foundation for thinking about ways of improving schools' (1996: 1) and the careers provision on offer to students.

Relationships and needs

As with many approaches to eliciting others' views, what was not said became an interesting focus. The student reports gave little evidence of their being consulted, and their learning needs being used to help plan the programme. Indeed, some comments indicated a considerable communications gap or distance between teachers and students.

> It [lessons] were quite patronising actually. I think they underestimate (. . . it's going to sound . . . I don't mean to sound stuck up, but) the average intelligence of the people that were doing it. I don't know who they were aiming for, but it was very patronising, some of the literature. There seemed to be little thought as to why we should do this, why it is important. (year 12)

In the new context of careers guidance interviews being handled by visiting careers officers, the lack of relationship and background knowledge with this occasional visitor came through.

> My careers interview was hopeless. He said, 'I don't know what to do for you!' And he said to me, he asked me what I thought my predicted grades would be, he asked me what I was interested in and I said, 'Law' and then he switched onto Politics and said 'well have you thought about being an MP?' I thought, well where did that come from, you know? (year 12)

> I didn't find mine [careers guidance interview] useful, because I didn't know what I wanted. (year 11)

Perhaps it would be surprising for anyone to be able to make such interviews meaningful for the student, although the encounter was sometimes valued for being challenging, rather than 'informative' or decisive.

The careers officer asked me really hard questions about why I wanted to study Arts management, it was really worthwhile. (year 12)

The different pattern of relationships which was experienced on work placements was remarked on.

Work experience taught me about working in teams, a lot about communication, it prepared you better than school for work. (year 11)

I didn't want to leave, they treated you like an adult, they expected things from me and I could do anything they asked. (year 10)

The overall picture of distance, possibly hierarchical distance, between 'planners' and 'receivers' mirrored the message in recent official documents. These focus on suggesting what is 'best' for the student in terms of what they need to know, understand and be able to do, but at no time do we hear the voice of the student, or any suggestion that students should be consulted in the planning process. There seemed to be little recognition of the 'social maturity of young people nor of the tensions and pressures they feel as they struggle to reconcile demands of their social and personal lives with the development of their identity as learners' (Rudduck *et al.* 1996).

TOWARDS AN ANALYSIS

Findings from an NFER survey (Stonet *et al.* 1998) paint a similar picture of students with little clear concept of what careers education was aiming at and little sense of coherence to the programme on offer. At one level it would be possible to conclude that a depressing picture has been painted of careers provision, and that the teachers and schools are to blame. In this sort of vein, a National Survey conducted for DfEE/OFSTED concluded in its key issues for action that there was a need for schools to 'plan the curriculum more effectively. Schools need to explain in much greater detail the nature, purpose and learning outcomes of their CEG programmes to staff, students and parents' (DfEE/OFSTED 1998: 8).

This, however, contains no mention of engaging the student perspective, and the risk is of reinforcing the very teacher-led provision which seems to be part of the problem. My work with students has certainly highlighted a mismatch between what national documents state about careers education and what actually happens in practice. Recently national documents and resource materials have focused on identifying the learning outcomes of careers work. Yet this could be a redundant exercise, unless both tutors and students have a shared view of what careers education is about, why they are doing it and its relevance to the rest of school curriculum and life beyond the classroom. This needs communication.

A focus on the communication between students and their careers teachers is indicated by my research. It also illuminates the tension in my own position. As a researcher and worker with the schools surveyed, I clearly have to be sensitive when 'feeding back' the student views which have been conveyed to me. Perhaps combining it with staff self-evaluation will help the process. But perhaps it is more important to explore the apparent lack of feedback from students to staff, and the lack of communication to identify student needs in career learning. This leads me to consider what position the staff seemed to be adopting.

THE CAREERS CO-ORDINATORS' VIEWS

Many of the staff I interviewed conveyed the view that the provision was good. This could have reflected that I was perceived as a hostile investigator, but I doubt it. It may have been related to a view of quality different from that of the students: for teachers, good quality careers work was well-organised careers work (despite a few doubts which had emerged):

> I believe short sharp career input is quite effective. It's very effective in years 9 and 11.

> I think the quality of what students get here is far superior [to what is on offer in other schools]. It is far better organised, far better structured. The main problem is we spoon-feed the kids too much and they take it for granted.

More general descriptions which co-ordinators offered reflected the received view from the conventional wisdom of official definitions:

> Careers is about raising student self-esteem and self-confidence and to prepare them for life-long career development.

> Careers is about telling students about job changes, that they're not going to have a job for life, there's no job security.

A lot of what we're aiming to do is for equal opportunities in terms of gender, race and sex.

Careers is about students making personal plans, setting targets and reviewing them.

Awareness was evident of the shortcomings of the traditional 'knowledge about jobs' approach.

Careers can motivate a child to work harder if they wish to enter certain professions by knowing what the academic requirements are. However, how long the motivation lasts I wouldn't like to say.

A distinct feature of the teacher talk was that it was phrased in terms of provision, 'we've done X', rather than in terms of students' needs, and the expectations of pupils were often low.

In year 9 we've done team-building and subject choice for key stage 4. In year 10 we concentrate on work experience. By Year 11 we encourage pupils to take responsibility for their own learning.

Howieson and Semple (1996), in a study of six Scottish secondary schools, noted that when asking teachers about students' guidance needs, the conversation quickly moved to one about provision. Reasons for this included a lack of any sustained attempt to evaluate pupils' needs. It was also sometimes the case that questions about needs were translated as pupils' 'problems' rather than their needs.

In these interviews, careers co-ordinators seemed to view parents as problems more often than as a resource:

It's very difficult because I'm afraid parents often turn round to me and say 'I want them to do Maths and English. Careers can take a back seat, and rightly so'.

We try to help pupils make the right decision, not to help parents make the right decision for their children.

Some co-ordinators had recognised that the lack of feedback questioned the quality of the programme.

What is going on in this Year 11 is probably not what should be going on but there is no time to really monitor it.

Overall, the picture painted by teachers felt very distant from that painted by students. One significant similarity emerged from their different accounts: neither party mentioned communicating with the other, either through feedback, or other communication to inform the design of the provision.

COULD IT BE DIFFERENT?

Even if the practice of these careers programmes is 'locked into a traditional and conventional approach that makes significant learning improbable if not impossible' (Rogers 1983: 21), I do think it could be otherwise. I believe that well-designed careers education has significant potential for being a key learning experience, but only if supported by high quality communication between teachers and students. Instead of mechanistic 'delivery', a focus on learning could emerge. Teachers' notion of 'provision' and 'coverage' is based on the assumption that what is taught is what is learnt; what is presented is what is assimilated. Careers learning needs to be seen as a personal developmental process, rather than simple knowledge acquisition. There is a need to use approaches which involve student participation and build on their experience beyond as well as within the classroom (Law and Knasel 1995). An approach to learning from experience (e.g. Dennison and Kirk 1990) would highlight the active learner (Do), the need for reflection and evaluation of learning experiences (Review), the extraction of meaning from the review (Learn) and the planned use of learning in future action (Apply).

Careers lessons have the potential to be challenging, questioning, critical, exciting, 'fun-filled' a real learning opportunity for both student and tutor. There are areas of work that students would like answers to, and careers lessons present the ideal forum. Tutors working alongside students are in a unique position to be asking students 'What do you want to learn? What things puzzle you? What are you curious about? What issues concern you? What problems do you wish you could solve?' (Rogers 1983: 136).

Rudduck *et al.* (1996) argue that neither policy-makers, government advisers nor teachers are planning the content, delivery, and monitoring of careers programmes with students. Perhaps it is because they do not credit pupils with the capacity to make constructive judgements of their schooling. Students are not only observant, but also capable of analytical and constructive comments. Their construction of careers and of themselves is developing fast, and 'it is vital that each individual "personal construct" of the world is explored' (Hoffbrand *et al.* 1998: 2/2).

Careers work requires that careers co-ordinators know or at least find out something about their students, not just about their school abilities, but their life experiences. Only by knowing something about their interests, goals, purposes, and passions can an effective careers programme be designed.

SO WHAT ABOUT FEEDBACK?

Student feedback is regularly described as a process which 'should inform the ongoing professional process of self-reflection, development and enhancement of learning and teaching. The fundamental purpose behind feedback is to enhance the quality of students' educational experience' (Loughborough 1998). This definition is interesting because it suggests that feedback is handled by the teacher, in a process whereby they improve the experience for the young person. This view of feedback encompasses a one-way process of communication, and could imply a passive or receptive view of learning. Although there are occasions when such a communication could lead to improvement, I feel it is probably limited, and would not sufficiently address the issue of relationships identified in the schools I surveyed.

Feedback should raise the question of what exactly young people are being taught, what they are expecting from their learning. In this way there may be a good chance that their views, experiences and needs drive the provision. I feel we need an expanded notion of feedback and its relation to learning. Feedback might then become communication about learning that is a two-way process, a co-constructive dialogue about learning; where students are active participants in the learning process. Power dynamics would also change, recognising that young people have a valuable contribution to make to the design and process of effective learning.

CONCLUDING REMARKS

Students' comments about careers education and guidance have cast doubt on some programmes, particularly where lessons are written as quick and easy activities from which all challenge and rigour has been removed. Many programmes patronise students with low expectations and do not engage them in activities in which they could make a real contribution and from which they could learn. The content of many careers activities implies that what students need to learn in order to manage their careers can be achieved without much thought or even sustained attention.

One of the findings from this study was that there is a need to learn more about differences between gender, race, class, life experiences, socio-economic experiences as well as the usual academic abilities of students. How students experience school, what it offers and how they view life in general. It is misleading to treat students as a homogeneous group, particularly when one considers the diversity that makes up the school population.

Whilst student feedback states that current practice is not working as well as it could be, it is too easy to apportion blame. Teachers involved in careers work need the chance to critically explore their own practice and develop a greater professionalism, alongside the structure and culture to create a much more communicative approach to practice.

REFERENCES

Dennison, B. and Kirk, R. (1990) *Do Review Learn Apply: a simple guide to experiential learning*, Oxford: Blackwell.

DfEE (1994) *Better Choices: the principles*, London: Department for Education and Employment.

DfEE (1997) White Paper *Excellence in Schools*, London: Stationery Office.

DfEE and OFSTED (1998) *National Survey of Careers Education and Guidance*, London: DfEE/OFSTED.

DTI (1994) White Paper *Competitiveness – Helping Business to Win*. London: Stationery Office.

Hoffbrand, J., MacDonald, J. and Thomas, C. (1998) *Careers Education and Guidance: what every teacher needs to know*. London: DfEE.

Howieson, C. and Semple, S. (1996) *Guidance in Secondary Schools*, Edinburgh: University of Edinburgh Centre for Educational Sociology.

Law, B. and Knasel, E. (eds) (1995) *Careers Work*, second edition, London: DfEE/HMSO.

Loughborough University Business School FDTL Project (1998) 'Student Feedback Systems'. Briefing Paper http: //www.lboro.ac.uk/departments/bs/fdtl.html.

Rogers, C. R. (1983) *Freedom to Learn*, Columbus OH: Charles E. Merrill.

Rudduck, J., Chaplain, R. and Wallace, G. (1996) *School Improvement: what can pupils tell us?*, London: David Fulton.

SCAA (1996) *Skills for Choice – developing pupils' career management skills for choice*, London: School Curriculum and Assessment Authority.

Stonet, S., Asby, P., Golden, S. and Lines, A. (1998) *Talking about Careers: young people's views of CEG at school*, London: NFER for Careers and Information Division, DfEE.

7 Learning from research

Felicity Wikeley[1]

INTRODUCTION

There have been many moves in the past few years to persuade the teaching profession that it needs to become a more research-based profession (Hargreaves 1996a). At the same time educational researchers have been accused of conducting irrelevant and poor quality research (Tooley 1998; Hillage *et al.* 1998). There obviously is a debate about the purposes of research and its relationship with practice but there is a growing rhetoric that the outcomes of educational research should be directly applicable to practice. Indeed research funding is increasingly dependent on user referees' comments. The reality for both researchers and practitioners is much more complex. Although teachers are being encouraged to conduct research in their own schools and classrooms (Hargreaves 1996b), the time to do this is problematic. During perhaps the greatest period of educational change with the introduction of new curricula, strategies and staff shortages even the most reflective practitioner will find it hard to create the time to also carry out research. Like teaching, research is a complex activity. It needs skills, time and motivation to be conducted effectively. Depending on its focus, it does not always have a neat application to classroom practice and can justifiably be more esoteric in nature. Research and teaching may be related but they are separate activities. It is not the purpose of this chapter to make the case for either teacher research or academic research but to explore how the outcomes of appropriate research can be shared with teachers in such a way as to enable them to make use of them. The problematic nature of this has been discussed elsewhere (Wikeley 1998) but this chapter explores how feedback can be incorporated into a research design with the aim of informing teachers' practice. It does not support any particular model of learning but explores the importance of creating opportunities for teachers to reflect on the purposes of their practice as well as the structures and strategies that support it.

The chapter uses the case of an evaluation by academic researchers of an action planning process implemented in Year 9 of schools in one LEA by a careers guidance company as part of the delivery of careers education. The intention was to develop an interactive research design, similar to that used in action research, which involved the researchers giving the teachers delivering the initiative feedback at all stages of the project in order to inform their practice.

The initiative was called Personal Learning Planning (PLP) and was described as a process which helped pupils recognise their academic and personal strengths and set targets for their own development. Its aims included:

- motivating and increasing self-confidence by involving pupils in planning their learning and development;
- ensuring that pupils regularly reviewed progress and set targets with tutors;
- supporting increased academic performance; and
- developing communication, negotiation and planning skills.

Central to the process was one-to-one or small group dialogue between the pupils and their tutors in Year 9. The title of the initiative emphasised its intention to promote pupils' understanding and confidence in their own learning, self-awareness and the development of their planning skills. But PLP was both a process and a product. The process supported pupils' learning through a focus on evidence about achievement and the identification of the pupils' own goals for improvement; while the product was an action plan, normally written by the pupil, which set out clear targets with appropriate action and times to achieve them.

The evaluation was to inform the development of the PLP initiative by identifying noteworthy practice and areas of strength and weakness and to gather evidence relating to the quality, impact and additionality of the process and the plans. A variety of data collection methods were used and central to these was the administration of a questionnaire to a cohort of approximately a thousand Year 9 pupils, from twenty-nine schools, at regular intervals throughout the last three years of their compulsory schooling. These questionnaires were to test the strength of feelings of the pupils about the fundamental issues relating to PLP (personal understanding, motivation, planning, target setting, talking to people, making choices, using the careers library, attitude to learning). The purpose of this chapter is not to discuss the pupil findings of the study (Bullock and Wikeley 1999a, b) but to discuss the feedback given to teachers and draw some conclusions as to the efficacy of the research design in promoting teachers' learning.

THE FEEDBACK PROCESS

Because it was intended that the evaluation should inform the development of the initiative in schools it was important that opportunities were created within the research design to discuss interim findings with the participating teachers. The key player in each school was seen to be the PLP co-ordinator and as a group they formed the primary audience for the feedback. As part of the main data collection the co-ordinator in each school was interviewed in the first and second year of the evaluation. These interviews were carried out by telephone and the co-ordinators were sent the interview schedule prior to being contacted at a convenient time. A second opportunity for feedback was created through conferences held each year which brought together the PLP co-ordinators and members of the schools' senior management teams to discuss interim findings with the research team and the project steering group. This group consisted of the careers guidance company PLP team, the DfEE manager (who were funding the project) and two headteacher representatives from the participating schools. Feedback was also used in the second phase of the research when case studies were conducted in eight of the participating schools as to how the process had developed and whether it was fulfilling its aims and objectives. These case studies involved focus group interviews with the PLP tutors of the original cohort and the tutors of the current Year 9 as well as PLP co-ordinators. With all three groups the researchers explored the findings from the pupil questionnaires as well as more general issues emerging from the whole data collection.

In the first year the interview questions were formulated to elicit the co-ordinator's view as to the way PLP was being implemented in the school and the constraints on that implementation. They were asked about the realities of the one-to-one discussion with pupils, the links with other initiatives, the role of the co-ordinator and the tutor training needs. The interviews were recorded and copies of the transcripts sent back to each co-ordinator for confirmation and amendment. The whole process was intended to give the co-ordinators maximum opportunity for reflection.

In the second year the interviews were customised to feed back to the school findings that were beginning to emerge for the questionnaire data. Again the co-ordinators were sent the questions prior to being contacted and they were asked specifically to discuss them with the tutors responsible for the delivery of the process. For example, the questionnaire data was analysed by school and gender and in some schools the process was found to be more effective with boys. The co-ordinators were asked to comment on particular trends in the data from their own pupils, when compared with the sample as a whole. They were asked for their interpretation of the findings and also about any particular aspects of the school's implementation that might have affected those outcomes.

Conferences were held at three points during the research process. The aim was to feed back specific findings from the analysis and to interrogate these with the practitioners in such a way as to inform the next stage of the evaluation as well as the development of the PLP process within the schools.

For eight of the twenty-nine schools there was a further phase of feedback which involved the compilation of case studies focusing on the longer-term effects of the PLP process. The aim of these case studies was to explore in more detail the factors, at school level, influencing the perceived effects of the PLP process and to discuss with the tutors as well as the co-ordinators, any particular aspects of the findings relating to their school. Although not reported here, pupils were also interviewed at this stage.

Although all three data collection methods had as one of their purposes to inform the next stage of the evaluation, they were predominantly a deliberate attempt at creating opportunities for the school staff to engage actively with the research findings as a way of informing their own learning.

THE FEEDBACK

At the first conference the PLP co-ordinators were split into groups with one member of the research team or steering group acting as facilitator and scribe. The senior managers formed a separate group with its own facilitator and scribe. Each group was asked to consider three questions:

1   What hard evidence might exist, now or in the future, to link PLP with effective learning?
2   What are effective organisational structures for sustaining and extending the PLP process in schools?

3   What does a quality Personal Learning Plan look like?

These three questions were chosen as being key issues arising from the first data collection but with hindsight they were also indicative of the level of knowledge and understanding needed by the schools to use the PLP process effectively. Although not planned as such they embody the focus of the feedback given over the subsequent two years. Consequently they are used in this chapter as the framework for the discussion of the feedback and its relationship with the teachers' learning.

The first question explored with the teachers the finding from the questionnaires that pupils were not seeing the PLP process as being connected with their learning. The DfEE, in funding the evaluation, wanted hard evidence (quantitative) as to the efficacy of the initiative in raising standards. One of the aims of the PLP process was to support increased academic performance. The researchers' intention was to use the feedback to explore both these issues with the teachers. As shown below, how the PLP process could support pupil learning became a vital question for all those involved in the process and was perhaps the most valuable lesson learned from the research. The feedback became an opportunity for the teachers to reflect on the purposes of the PLP process in a similar way to their engagement with the pupils in reflecting on their learning. Perceptions of the purposes of PLP were quite influential in how the initiative was being delivered and exploring these was an important learning experience for all those involved.

The careers guidance company also envisaged that PLP would dovetail into similar processes in Years 10 and 11 (e.g. National Record of Achievement, Progress File). From the interviews it was apparent that this coincided with the schools' views but to varying effect. The second question was to help them address concerns about how continuity might be enhanced and sustained. As the original research cohort progressed through the school, other Year 9 cohorts were experiencing the PLP process. The case study interviews with the current Year 9 tutors, exposed misunderstandings in their thinking about its purposes that were likely to influence its sustainability and relationship with other initiatives.

The PLP initiative had as one of its outcomes the production of an action plan by each pupil that included targets for future learning. The careers guidance company provided the documentation for this although its format had been developed in consultation with the schools. The third question wanted the groups to articulate what they considered a good PLP document would look like and how important a part of the process they considered it to be. From the pupil questionnaires and the interviews it was apparent that there was some tension between views of PLP as a process and PLP as product. This tension was played out at all levels during the feedback.

LEARNING OUTCOMES

Linking PLP with effective learning

For many attending the conference the discussion of the first question initially focused on what counted as 'hard evidence'. Many felt that often outcomes of effective learning were not measurable in the quantifiable sense and this created conflict for the co-ordinators. The view was also expressed that there had to be some shared understanding as to what counted for 'learning' before evidence could be accepted or rejected. Helping co-ordinators explore this issue became a major part of the feedback process. Although the PLP process was founded on a notion of helping pupils become more autonomous learners, there was clearly some contention amongst the teachers as to what that might mean. The following were suggested as evidence that might be used to show PLP was promoting effective learning and illustrated this conflict:

- improved examination/SAT results preferably using some notion of value-added;
- destinations information;
- pupils making better/more informed choices at Y11, of work experience, options, careers;
- better quality careers office/guidance interviews;
- better quality National Records of Achievement being produced; and
- pupils initiating the use of careers resources and the frequency of usage.

These all show an outcomes, external objectives view of learning. The following indicate a more personal, developmental view of learning:

- raised self-esteem/self-confidence;
- improved ability in meeting and communicating their short-term goals;
- improved ability in assessing and articulating strengths and weaknesses and setting realistic goals in all areas (personal/social academic/vocational);

- improved interpersonal skills – individual and group, peers, tutor, parents/guardians, subject staff; and
- more positive reporting, fewer sanctions.

Although both views are valid, the question of which could most usefully be addressed by the PLP process was a recurring theme. It was the debate about the purposes of the process and its relationship with different aspects of learning that dominated all future discussion about the feedback from the project. In the interviews in the second year the issue was explored further with individual co-ordinators. They were asked about changes that they had made in the preceding year in response to the research findings. They were asked if there were any changes in the schools' KS3 results that might be attributable to PLP; for their explanations of the effects of PLP with particular groups of pupils; and if the emerging finding, that pupils were still seeing PLP as an aid to making choices rather than as an aid to their own learning, resonated with their own experience.

There was some debate about whether or not improvement in examination or test results could be attributed to any individual intervention. The complexity of pupils' lives (Rudduck *et al.* 1996) both in and out of school makes it extremely difficult to claim any causal link. Making connections between a process that was focused on involving pupils in their learning and the increasing expectation in schools for improved performance was a real point of tension for the teachers, particularly for the tutors delivering the process. This tension was often expressed in terms of the uneasy relationship between PLP targets and more subject-oriented targets.

However, from the interviews it was clear that the teachers were positive about the value of the one-to-one interviews in Year 9. There was some evidence that boys, more than girls, gained more directly from the one-to-one discussion with their tutor which the co-ordinators suggested was partly a function of the earlier maturing and skills of reflection in adolescent girls. At age thirteen boys entered PLP with greater reluctance to analyse and plan their lives and the impact of the one-to-one conversation with a tutor may, therefore, have been more significant. The co-ordinators reported that tutors felt that the dialogue helped them to get to know pupils quicker and better. This had nurtured positive relationships between staff and pupils. Particular benefits mentioned were that the PLP interview distinguished the relatively quiet group of average attainers, provided quicker support strategies for those who were struggling and made identification of specific needs easier.

You don't know them very well until one-to-one.

However there was very little reporting of how tutors had explored strategies for learning with the pupils. Co-ordinators felt that as a result of PLP more Year 9 pupils had given thought to their future, where they wanted to be and what they needed to get there and there was some evidence from the questionnaire that the PLP dialogue raised boys' skills and confidence in thinking and talking about their own strengths and weaknesses. For some, conducting an individual conversation with an adult outside the family was a real step forward in communication skills.

At first they won't even look an adult in the eye and are struggling to get words out, but at the end of it they're actually making eye contact, talking more confidently.

However, the evidence pointed to a gap between the perceptions of tutors, and the perceptions of the pupils for whom it was primarily a school process about making option choices. This is not to say that they did not enjoy talking with their tutors; they just failed to see the wider learning benefits. From the case study interviews it was apparent that there were also some tutors who had not made this connection.

The second conference therefore focused on the relationship between PLP and learning. The researchers presented the ongoing findings from the questionnaires and also related the initiative to other research on learning. The presentation reviewed research into learning and the way people learn and focused on what teachers need to know about learning (MacGilchrist *et al.* 1997). The PLP process was considered from its role in enabling teachers to be:

- knowledgeable about learning as a process (Abbott 1994);
- knowledgeable about learners;
- knowledgeable about what learners want (Rudduck *et al.* 1996).

Small group discussion centred on how the process could be more related to pupil learning and how all staff in the school, not just the tutors delivering the process, could be involved. For example, subject tutors were setting academic targets with pupils but if the tutor was to have a key role in helping the pupil achieve those targets, helping them make connections between the different subject targets through identification of more generic learning issues, could be important. Involving subject teachers in the PLP process so that they became aware that subject targets were not being set in isolation, was also important.

Sustaining and extending the PLP process in schools

Discussion of the second question highlighted the need to embed the process in the culture of the school. Although the schools were implementing the same initiative, the need for a flexible approach adapted to suit individual school needs was important. The process had to be part of the school ethos and valued by all, particularly senior staff, and including parents. This was a particularly relevant issue for those co-ordinators who were still seeing PLP as a careers service initiative. For these schools the process was still seen as separate from other initiatives and closely connected with careers choice rather than concerned with developing pupil attitudes to learning. The opportunity to explore this with others involved in the same initiative, ensured that the feedback was not viewed as criticism but as part of their own reflection on the process. Discussing a whole range of alternatives in how other schools were structuring the process helped them see that there was not one 'right' way of proceeding. Co-ordinators and senior managers were able to reflect on the real advantages of PLP and how it could be used effectively rather than feeling they had failed to meet some externally imposed objectives. By creating the opportunity for the co-ordinators to discuss the possibility of a flexible approach meant that their own school circumstances were not ignored. It also enabled their particular constraints to be acknowledged in the research report.

For example, the tutor's role needed to be recognised although each school needed to work out its own operational system. Tutors needed time to carry out the process effectively, for example, by time-tabling PLP interviews so that subject teaching time was not disrupted. Sometimes a goodwill gesture, e.g. allowing teachers to work flexitime, was enough to acknowledge the increased intrusion into non-contact time. The financial support provided by the careers guidance company was considered necessary for the provision of good quality support materials, resources and supply cover (considered essential). Financial support allowed the increased use of IT (e.g. e-mail, information databases) and the use of personal organisers for the collation of targets and achievements. An accessible recording system was also considered important in order that pupils maintained ownership of the process and some schools had developed quite innovative approaches to this.

The need for PLP to become embedded in the school culture also

raised issues of communication and continuity. The co-ordinators identified a need to establish links between Y9, 10 and 11, pupil/tutor
feedback to subject leaders, and coherence and integration with other
initiatives. Some schools had already attempted to create structured
ways of doing this and contextualising the PLP process in other
research on learning was felt to be a helpful way of introducing it to
other staff. The need to have a view of the big picture if learning is to
be seen to be relevant was realised to be important. For example, Biggs
and Moore's (1993) description of effective learning emphasises the
need for monitoring and regular review. The tutors interviewed in the
case studies felt that there was very little opportunity in some schools
in the PLP process for revisiting targets and reviewing progress.
Similarly there was little opportunity given in some schools for tutors
to review the process and their own learning in relation to it. A need
for tutors' learning processes to mirror those in which they were engaging their pupils began to emerge.

Process or product?

This was an important debate that continued throughout the project.
Was the value of PLP the final document or the process?

> There is no quality PLP.
> Process is more important than quality [document].
> The Personal Learning Plan is only valid at end of Y 9 (life moves
> on!).

For some the outcomes of the process (the document) showed that the
pupils had understood what the process was about. The final document
needed to be legible, needed to be seen as a record of a particular time
in the pupil's life, be part of a wider collection of material from PSE etc.
and written in a language which was forward-looking and developmental but a standard form gave credibility to the process. A quality
document would show *realism from individual pupils* and would have
meaning to individual pupils – personalisation. Such documents would
show increased personal responsibility and realistic targets that were
possible for subject teachers and tutors to follow up. In other words it
needed to be seen to be implemented. This was not always apparent in
some schools.

However, some tutors expressed frustration at the process being
document led. In some schools the process appeared centred on the
completion of the document. The meeting between the pupil and tutor

did not occur until the document was written in draft and the one-to-one dialogue focused on the document, the personal statement and the targets set be the pupil. In some cases pupils regarded this as a marking process which emphasised for them the school-directed nature of PLP. For example in one school there was clearly some conflict about the meaning of 'achievement'. For the tutors achievement equalled publicly recognised events (e.g. medals for dancing) but for some pupils it also could include more personal learning (e.g. learning to cope with parents' divorce). The tutor had returned the document with the 'achievement' section crossed out and a suggestion that the pupil recorded her prizes. This illustrated the need for a common understanding as to the real purposes of the process.

Those who regarded PLP as a process viewed the plan itself as a working document and only one part of the process of recording achievements and target setting. Others felt a quality process showed a co-ordinated approach by the school so that the pupils could see progression rather than repetition. It was about promoting the discourse between pupils, teachers, parents, and careers advisers.

CONCLUSIONS

The aim of the chapter was to explore the lessons that could be learnt from researchers giving regular feedback to practitioners from a project in which they were actively involved. One lesson is perhaps that learning cannot always be planned. Perhaps a timely lesson for those implementing an initiative aimed at helping young people plan their learning. However, this chapter is specifically about teachers and what they can learn from being involved in a research process.

One interesting finding from the feedback process was the mirroring of the process, if not the content, experienced by the teachers with that of their pupils. PLP was a process by which pupils could, with the support of their tutors, reflect on evidence of their learning in such a way as to enable them to plan it more effectively. Feedback from the research enabled teachers, with the support of the researchers, to reflect on their practice in such a way as to help them plan it more effectively. What it exposed was that some teachers needed time to reflect on the theoretical underpinnings of that practice. In engaging with the researchers through the feedback, opportunities for practitioners to reflect on more than the implementation differences of the initiative were created. For the teachers, whether co-ordinators or tutors, the possibility of discussing their understanding of the concept of learning in the context of the PLP aims, proved to be very important. Research reports that focus on the factors influencing the effectiveness of the process are unlikely to get beyond the 'we do that' or 'we don't do that' form of engagement. Feedback from the careers guidance company's quality assurance visits was likely to have a similar effect. The fact that the researchers had been given the brief of taking an overview and were presenting the individual school findings within that context, enabled the teachers to view their own situation from a broader perspective. Putting the research findings in the context of wider research on learning had a similar effect. Until the practitioners had had the opportunity to explore the possibilities of the PLP process in its entirety, many had found it difficult to see beyond its option choice connection.

Using feedback within the research also enabled the careers guidance company to address these broader issues. They had developed the PLP initiative within the context of new thinking about careers education and the move away from careers choice to engagement with broader transferable skills. Engaging with the teachers' less developed understanding of the change gave them an insight into future staff development needs. It also helped them understand that tutor involvement in the initiative did not necessarily imply a complete understanding of its purposes or that their (the careers guidance company) purposes were matched by the perceptions of those who delivering it (the tutors). From the case study interviews it was apparent that tutors as well as the co-ordinators needed to be part of the feedback process. Joyce *et al.* (1999) use the concept of the evolutionary school to describe how schools need to build community as well as a knowledge base. Building community was still an issue for the careers guidance company as well as for many of the schools in the initiative. The assumptions about meanings, purpose and values need to be explored at a deep level with everyone involved.

Finally, the reality for the teachers in schools cannot be ignored. The lesson for the researchers was that when using feedback with teachers they must show a clear understanding of that reality. The data belong to the researchers but just as parents want to recognise their own child in her/his school report, the teachers must recognise their own practice in the data, even if the purpose of the feedback is to change that practice. The context of the school has to be evident. The culture of the staff cannot be ignored. Teachers can become understandably defensive if they feel that their practice is being criticised when they are working within parameters that are not of their making. The real advantage of this feedback process was its presentation as a

two-way process capable of commenting on the constraints of implementation as well as the strengths of the initiative.

NOTE

1 The research reported in this chapter was jointly directed by the author and
Kate Bullock of University of Bath. The author would like to acknowledge
the help and support given by Kate in the writing of the chapter.

REFERENCES

Abbott, J. (1994) *Learning Makes Sense: re-creating education for a changing
future*, Letchworth: Education 2000.

Biggs, J. B. and Moore, P. J. (1993) *The Process of Learning*, Englewood
Cliffs, NJ: Prentice Hall.

Bullock, K. and Wikeley, F. (1999a) 'Improving learning in Year 9: making use
of personal learning plans', *Educational Studies* 25:1, 19–33.

Bullock, K and Wikeley, F. (1999b) 'Personal Learning Plans: supporting students' learning', paper presented to conference of British Educational
Research Association, University of Sussex.

Hargreaves, D. (1996a) 'Teachers, educational research and evidence-based
teaching' *Education Review* 10:2, 46–50.

Hargreaves, D. H. (1996b) 'Teaching as a Research-based Profession: possibilities and prospects', Teacher Training Agency Annual Lecture.

Hillage, J., Pearson, R., Anderson, A. and Tamkin, P. (1998) *Excellence in
Research on Schools*, London: Department for Education and Employment.

Joyce, B., Calhoun, E. and Hopkins, D. (1999) *The New Structure of School
Improvement: inquiring schools and achieving students*, Buckingham: Open
University Press.

MacGilchrist, B., Myers, K. and Reed, J. (1997) *The Intelligent School*,
London: Paul Chapman.

Rudduck, J., Chaplain, R. and Wallace, G. (1996) *School Improvement: what
can pupils tell us?*, London: David Fulton.

Tooley, J. (1998) *Educational Research: a critique, a survey of published educational research*, London: Office for Standards in Education.

Wikeley, F. (1998) 'Dissemination of research: a tool for school improvement?',
School Leadership and Management 18:1, 59–73.

8 Communications between school and home – correction, consultation or conversation for learning?

Susan Askew

INTRODUCTION

I am a parent and was a secondary school teacher for fifteen years. My interest in communications between schools and home arises from my experiences; as a parent I often felt anxious, defensive, guilty, angry or merely relieved when talking to teachers! As a teacher I also often felt anxious, defensive or relieved when talking to parents. This interest led to a research project with parents of primary and secondary age children. It explores their experiences of communication with teachers. All parents live and work in London and are female. Their occupations cover a broad spectrum of professional and semi-skilled work. The central research questions were:

- What are parents' experiences of communication between school and home?
- What do parents perceive the purpose of communication between school and home to be?

I start by giving examples of communication which parents found useful, followed by an analysis of issues relating to parents' evenings. All parents, apart from one who had a daughter in a private school, were more critical than positive about communication between school and home. I present their major concerns and continue by analysing parents' perceptions of the purpose of communication from school.

I argue that parents' experiences reflect a dominant model of communication from teachers to parents which has giving information for reassurance or 'correction' as its main purpose. I suggest from the evidence that conversations between school and home are rare. An alternative model is offered based on dialogue. This facilitates learning for the young person, parent and teachers.

WHAT ARE PARENTS' EXPERIENCES OF COMMUNICATION FROM SCHOOL?

Examples of good practice

All parents talk positively about school reports which are usually detailed and informative. Three parents contrast their child's reports with their own:

> I was looking at my own reports. There's about 20 words for the whole report, including marks out of 10, reading age, or some cursory comment about behaviour. Amazing documents. Then I looked at my daughter's reports – the amount of work that had gone into them, at the detail and the comments they have against National Curriculum targets. I thought about the amount of time it must have taken to specify where she had got to, as well as the more detailed social commentary about who she is. I don't know how they do it. (parent of 13-year-old girl)

Parents welcome informal occasions to meet staff and mention newsletters which they find useful:

> There's a parents' evening once a year which is normally the first term so you get to know the teachers early on, and that's preceded by a social group meeting for all the parents so that you get to know the parents – it's a get together, informal and social. The parents' evening is one to one. They give a newsletter termly and the updates in between are excellent. I don't know if this is typical but it's typical in my experience of that kind of school. (parent of 12-year-old girl – private school)

A surprising number of parents were asked to go into the school specifically to talk about a problem (approximately 80 per cent). Parents stress that *useful* communications about problems include the child. These revolve around problem-solving and agreeing short-term goals together:

> My daughter was involved in discussions. That was handled very well to the school's credit. It's rare I think. They were consistent and supportive in trying to broker a new arrangement. That worked out eventually. (parent of 15-year-old girl)

One parent contrasts a negative experience where her daughter was asked to leave her secondary school, with her subsequent experience in the next school where a satisfactory outcome for her daughter was achieved. Parents compare strategies which work with those which do not:

> She was quite a troublesome child. They couldn't wait to get rid of her. She went to (. . . school) after that and she was still difficult but they were just so understanding and caring and really tried to help. It was 'Let's have a look at the situation. Let's see what we can do', and in the meetings 'Why do you think you're doing these things?' There was more discussion and negotiation. It was human and not patronising either the child or me. (parent of 17-year-old girl)

Parents comment that useful strategies involve interaction. The second quote below illustrates that feedback should be two-way and should involve conversation:

> The best ones say: 'I am working on a strategy to get your child to do this and it would be good if you could do this'. Actually tell you the educational aims and give you the sort of information you might need to try and support what is going on. Ask you what you suggest. (parent of 14-year-old boy)

> I like the fact they ask you to write back and comment. That's really good. I know that's asking a lot to ask teachers to take that on, but feedback should go back the other way as well, it should be a conversation it strikes me. (parent of 15-year-old girl)

Only the parent with a daughter in a private school suggests that she can set up meetings, with the implication that she can also negotiate the agenda:

> They have an open door policy. You can always phone or make an appointment for a chat. The school is quite small. It's wonderful. I wish I had a schooling like that. (parent of 12-year-old girl – private school)

It would appear that if the school is asking a parent to come in, they are implicitly responsible for setting the agenda.

Comments on parents' evenings

Many writers have previously noted that parents' evenings do not work for either parents, teachers or young people: 'Parents evenings are an ordeal. In many cases this is true for both parents and teachers alike, not to mention the pupils' (Horne 1999). Other studies of parents' evenings also indicate feelings of dissatisfaction (Clark and Power 1998; Walker 1998). None of the parents in my research talked positively about parents' evenings, and many talked about lack of privacy:

> I have never liked the structure of parents' evenings. In the first year you would go into the classroom of the year tutor and there would be other parents and children in the classroom. I wanted to have a private conversation which I thought was more helpful and I recall the teachers being surprised at this. Later they moved to a system where the teachers sat around the hall so we would come in and mill around and go and sit in a queue. I thought this was badly managed. An appointment system would be better. (parent of 16-year-old boy)

Parents also complain that parents' evenings are one-way exchanges:

> It's a difficult way of communicating. Teachers are tired, it's the end of a long day, and if you see them at the end, their ability to give any useful information is long gone and my ability to absorb any useful information is long gone. Maybe a letter to me and an arrangement to talk in a different way would be more useful. I'd like more of a chance to say what I think – I could tell them some useful things about my daughter. (parent of 15-year-old girl)

Other writers (Todd 1998; Walker and MacLure 1999) have commented on the imbalance of power between teachers and parents:

> In such talk, the balance of power is generally seen as favouring the 'professional' over the 'client'. Teachers had the right to speak first and at some length, and thus to define what would count as 'legitimate' topics for the consultation.
> (Walker and MacLure 1999: 1)

Walker and MacLure suggest that teachers exercise a range of subtle control strategies, including control over the flow of personal information; control over the definition of the problem; control over follow-up actions. They comment:

Communication with parents receives very little explicit attention during pre- and in-service teacher education. There is a need for educational programmes to redress this situation. It is only by understanding the complex negotiations over power and identity that take place during these five minute encounters that teachers and parents will be able to work towards more equitable home school 'partnerships'.

(Walker and MacLure 1999: 2)

Identifying concerns

Parents identify various concerns relating to communication, summarised in Table 8.1.

Table 8.1 Concerns raised by parents

Concern	Example
Contact only made when something is going wrong	Children say it's not fair 'They never tell you when I'm being good, only when I'm being bad'. It's always negative. The only time you get any positive feedback is on the reports because it's then the teacher says 'Has done well this term – has tried hard', but that's only in written form on the report. (parent of 15-year-old boy)
Less useful communication in secondary than primary school because of more emphasis on relationships in primary schools	In primary you collect them, there's more face-to-face contact, more opportunity to talk. In secondary you don't go into school unless you have to. In primary when I collect my son the teacher says, 'Oh I'm very pleased with [son's name] today, he did this or this'. So they hear the teacher as well. (parent of 7-year-old boy)
Negative patterns of communication because of target setting and a focus on examination performance	The whole context of education currently is fraught with anxiety, kids, teachers and parents' performance. It's worse in secondary school. There's the idea that if you don't get your 5 A-C GCSE you are going to drop into this hole called social exclusion and you are never going to be able to recover from that. And I find myself being affected by it. I think good communication is so difficult because there's so much anxiety about. (parent of 15-year-old girl)
	Things have changed over the 12 years I have had children in school. Teachers have less time.

Table 8.1 cont.

Concern	Example
	There's been a shift from the pastoral side to the academic side. There aren't so many social things in schools any more for kids and parents to join in. I think even the teachers have less social time together. Also the kids are doing SATS now even in primary school. (parent of 16-year-old boy)
Relationships with parents from some ethnic minority groups	I think the relationship between the parents of black children, particularly black boys, and the school are sometimes bad, because I think they are often viewed as problems. (parent of 17-year-old boy)
Teachers' perceptions of parents	I am astounded at the negative view of parents that is held by virtually all of the staff in the school. I was having a conversation with some teachers in the school recently and every time they referred to parents talking they used the word 'gossip' until I intervened. I pointed out that parents talking in the playground is legitimate. (parent of 7-year-old boy)
	Parents are viewed negatively as a hazard to children's education. I think if the child is doing well this is not a problem but as soon as there is a problem of any kind it is. (parent of 16-year-old boy)
Lack of communication skills	Some parents are difficult, there is no question. But one of the skills that professional teachers have to have is the skill to deal with such people. What's really professional is dealing with the people who are angry and are upset. I think there's a tradition that goes right through the school from the beginning that parents are not particularly important or are a negative influence, not that good communication with them is positive. (parent of 15-year-old girl)
Authoritarian structures and lack of negotiation	Authoritarian practitioners no matter what sort of child they have in front of them, operate straight up and down on the dubious notion that you treat everybody the same. With the result that children who are more wilful, not easily intimidated, quite enjoy the challenge. I think there's a whole group of feisty young women

Table 8.1 cont.

Concern	Example
	who challenge authority all the time. Saying you do it this way or that way doesn't work. Negotiate. She likes being treated as an individual. She does not give respect as a matter of course, it's got to be earned. She's not deferential. (parent of 16-year-old girl)
Lack of partnership	We have discussed how the school communicates with parents and there is a great deal of lip service to government speak about partnerships and this sort of thing, but from my experience on the ground it does not exist (parent of 17 -year-old boy)
	There's the whole school contract part. I think they are fascinating documents in their own right. It seems to me that the commitment is being placed and enjoined on parents to sign into a very specific commitment. It's all about parents must get their children to school on time, wear uniform. The school says 'we will ensure that we offer your child the best opportunities'. All very vague. (parent of 16-year-old girl)

WHAT DO PARENTS PERCEIVE THE PURPOSE OF FEEDBACK FROM TEACHERS TO BE?

Since the early 1970s there have been arguments for increased parental involvement in school and stress on the home–school 'partnership'.

Attempts to work more closely with parents followed from research highlighting the importance of experiences at home in the achievement of young people in school (Tizard and Hughes 1984; Athey 1990) as well as about ways to increase the accountability of schools to parents. It seems from talking to parents that there are few occasions where communications between home and school focus on *how* this partnership can support the young person's learning. Parents of primary age children are more likely to talk about practical ways in which this partnership may work and to mention communications that appear to have this aim:

My son's school is marvellous. They give us information on flash cards and how to use them at home, and they tell us about the homework. The flash cards are to help; with reading. They also have a homework agreement that all parents sign so you feel you are committed to it. (parent of 8-year-old boy)

However, the goal of most communications from school to home is not clear, nor is it clear how parents can make use of communications to support their child's learning. This raises the question of what the purpose of the communication is. Many parents I interviewed see the goals of written communication about work as either to reassure, or to draw attention to problems:

I think the purpose of the reports is reassurance if the child is able, but also to signal any concerns. (parent of 12-year-old girl)

When a problem has been identified, parents talk about what they assume is expected of them:

The idea is I think that the parents get so fed up that they get on to the children. If they badger the parents enough they will make sure children get there on time, with the correct equipment and school uniform. (parent of 14-year-old boy)

None of the parents interviewed had instigated a meeting with teachers because of their own concerns. Some parents asked to come into school to discuss problems seem to experience a feeling of helplessness, or blame:

They asked me to go into the school several times. I remember sitting with his form teacher, head of year and deputy head, all men. I felt quite intimidated. They were telling me that he refused to do as he was told and made up his own rules. I basically felt bad because I couldn't get him to school on time or to do his homework. (parent of 14-year-old boy)

Teachers may hope that by telling parents about children's anti-social behaviour, or lack of effort and motivation, the parent will be able to make their child conform to expectations. In some cases this may appear to work:

In my opinion they expect us to talk to the child, tell them they can't watch TV or something like that. But I believe in smacking as well and he's behaving himself in school now. (parent of 6-year-old boy)

However, the belief that the parent can discipline the child or make them do as they are told clearly causes problems and does not support children in developing their own coping strategies.

I talk to him. It's why haven't you got your books, make sure you have them tomorrow. I suppose it works. But then we get annoyed with him and he gets annoyed with us, then he gets annoyed with the teachers for telling us. But at the end of the day he does turn up with his books.

Q: And the next day?

Well, it works for a little while. But he's a teenage boy, I can't get him to pick his clothes up in the bedroom. And at the end of the day you can't stand there every morning and say, have you got your books, because he has to learn to take responsibility for himself. (parent of 14-year-old)

One issue in relation to learning is the extent to which responsibility for experiences and for learning is encouraged. Taking responsibility for others can be disempowering and gives implicit messages about lack of ability. A further problem with trying to help someone else avoid the consequences of their behaviour is that they do not learn how to deal successfully with difficult situations in their lives – their coping strategies remain underdeveloped. This point is related to the comments of one parent who talked about her daughter's struggle for independence and autonomy:

My daughter is struggling for autonomy and control and increasingly resents any boundaries or injunctions we place on her. And into this fairly toxic situation where she's trying to be independent there's the school and there's us. Obviously sometimes we align with the school because we are worried, so it's very hard to do well in a way that makes people feel things are possible after a communication. Sometimes you feel a bit of despair. (parent of a 16-year-old girl)

Surprisingly, half of the parents interviewed talk about the amount of contact from school over issues, which they felt the school should deal with directly.

They'll be on the phone straight away – at home or work or on the mobile to track you down. 'He hasn't been behaving too well today, or he hasn't turned up for a lesson'. Even more mundane things, like 'He didn't bring his equipment to the math's lesson today' or 'He's wearing trainers not shoes'. The school should deal with minor things. (parent of 14-year-old boy)

The underlying message is that it is a parent's responsibility to make sure that their child behaves correctly. This may seem a perfectly reasonable expectation, and yet trying to change someone else's behaviour is problematic. Young people are more likely to keep to school rules if they have been involved in deciding them and are clear about their rationale.

Parents' views on communication between school and home seem to illustrate a particular model of relationship which MacBeth (1989) calls 'containment' and which I have adapted and call the 'correction' approach. The following section critically reviews this model. I argue that communication between home and school should draw more heavily on the features, which I outline in two other models of relationships between home and school – consultation and collaboration (developed from the work of MacBeth 1989 and Askew and Carnell 1996).

THE DOMINANT MODEL OF COMMUNICATION FROM TEACHERS TO PARENTS

Correction

I argue there is a dominant model of communication, which I call 'correction'. In this model there is limited and formal contact with parents. Parents are not consulted. Communication is one-way, from school to home. Parents have little access to the building, records, teachers or the curriculum. Contact is likely to be limited to parents' evenings or to tell parents about problems with work or behaviour.

Keogh (1996: 130) argues that 'parents are instructed in what to do, how to see, being positioned as adjunct teachers'. Other writers (Crozier 1998) have argued that communication in this model appears to be for the purpose of surveillance and social control over the home. Research (Bastiani 1988; Walker 1998) has found that parents and teachers have mismatched expectations, mutual incomprehension; the rules of engagement and role of participants are unclear.

As my research indicates, feedback given in this mode may be based on stereotypical assumptions about parents and young people. The correction model is likely to reinforce misconceptions and misunderstanding since there is no room in this approach for exploration of meaning and difference. For example, the view that parents lack concern for their children's education or are apathetic. Research since the 1980s has indicated that the majority of parents *are* concerned (Marland 1983; MacBeth 1989, Tizard *et al.* 1988). However, some parents are hesitant and unsure of themselves when confronted by the systems of schooling (Johnson and Ransom 1983). Marland wrote:

> the huge majority of parents are not apathetic but very concerned, . . . the nature of their concerns and the modes of their support have a great deal to teach us teachers.
>
> (Marland 1983: 4)

Wolfendale's research (1992) illustrates a variety of reasons why parents should be more involved in school:

- All parents care about their children's welfare and well-being (the tiny minority who appear not to care do so either because of stress in their lives or because their own experience of schooling was negative and left them with fears and anxieties about school).
- Parents want to do what they believe to be in their child's best interests.
- Parents want to co-operate.
- Parents will respond to invitations to participate in school if they can see the benefit to their child.
- Parents are the primary educators of their children and are experts on their children.
- Parent and teacher skills complement one another.
- Parents often have vital information and insights concerning their children.
- Involvement of parents should include decision-making, not simply information giving.
- All parents have a right to be involved and to contribute.

A correction view of relationships between school and home is congruent with particular views of learning. When 'correction' is the primary motive for communication, it is more likely that the underlying approach to learning in the school is one which is referred to as the 'reception-transmission' approach to learning (Carnell, Askew and Lodge – this volume). In the reception–transmission approach to learning teachers are 'the experts'. Learners are viewed as passive recipients of knowledge and information. Similarly, in the 'correction' model of home–school relationships parents are viewed as passive recipients of information and teachers do not usually know whether this information is useful. In the reception–transmission approach the goals for learning are not negotiated and are set by the teacher or by education policy makers.

In the reception–transmission approach there is an imbalance of power between teacher and child or parent:

> Power is both implicit and explicit in relationships between parents and professional educators even in situations where both parties have a common goal in supporting the education of a child.
>
> (Todd and Higgins 1998: 235)

The power of the 'expert' may have worked for both teacher and parent in the past, but Todd and Higgins (1998) also suggest that professionals now need the opportunity to have 'a less fixed view of themselves and their role to allow a flexible mutuality between parents and teachers'. Such a view is possible in the consultation and collaborative models.

Consultation

In this model there is some commitment to developing a partnership with parents and recognition that this is important for young people's learning. Parents may be asked for their advice or for information, and there is more negotiation. Communication is more informal and there is likely to be an 'open door' policy in the school. However, the agenda for discussion between school and parents is usually identified by the school.

As in the correction model, the teachers primarily see themselves as 'experts'. However, it is recognised that parents also have expertise and have something to offer the school, rather than, in the words of one parent in my research 'being a hazard to their child's education'. Young people are more central in discussions and it may also be recognised that they have some expertise in relation to knowledge about their own learning.

Parallels can be drawn between the consultation model and the constructivist approach to learning discussed by Askew and Lodge (this volume). In the constructivist approach there is a stress on making connections and developing meaning. Feedback in the constructivist approach involves the teacher in description and discussion rather than evaluation. In this form of feedback the 'expert' helps the learner construct understanding, and solve problems. Several comments from parents indicate the view that useful communication has features in common with the constructivist approach to learning; they stress joint goal setting, problem solving, and interaction. Consultation with parents is a step towards 'communication' between home and school, which is discussed in the third model of home–school relationships – collaboration.

Collaboration

In the collaborative model it is recognised that schools have an important role in developing some aspects of the child's learning and that learning outside of school is equally important. In a collaborative relationship neither teachers nor parents are viewed as the experts on young people's learning; teachers, parents and young people are seen as learning together. Each is an expert on their own learning and can give useful feedback to one another. Collaboration involves working together on joint goals.

The UNESCO report on education for the twenty-first century argues for collaboration in education as a means towards a more equitable society:

> While education is an on-going process of improving knowledge and skills, it is also, perhaps primarily, an exceptional means of bringing about personal development and building relationships among individuals, groups and nations.
>
> (UNESCO 1996: 14)

This vision of collaborative relationships in society may start with the introduction of small, manageable change, for example, by identifying existing relationships between school and parents and building on good practice.

I argue that collaborative relationships must be based on co-construction approaches. This suggests the idea of learning dialogues in which the participants are all learners. In this process relationships are central. Co-construction implies a two-way exchange and involves a shift in perception of young people, teachers and parents and their roles.

In a collaborative model, it is assumed that parents and teachers have the same goals, but the goals of learning themselves need to be discussed as part of the dialogue. It seems pertinent to end with a quote from one parent, which sums up one important finding:

> When children are compliant and fit in the system communication isn't an issue. It's not visible, but when children have any problems how it's handled is really crucial. (parent of 16-year-old girl)

This highlights a surprising aspect of my research. I did not set out to interview parents who had experienced difficult communication with school, this was a random sample. Many parents talked about their children being perceived as problematic. Where there were problems there were difficulties in communicating. Such difficulties are based on particular assumptions about learning which do not recognise that communications between home and school are opportunities for learning. The dominant form of feedback to parents fits with Askew and Lodge's notion (this volume) of 'feedback as a gift'. The question is, however, is the gift appropriate, is it wanted and what is to be done with it!

I am left with a conundrum. I am writing about feedback from parents and, like all written communication, this fits with reception–transmission views of teaching and learning – another 'gift'. Yet I am arguing for co-construction approaches. I hope my readers will be able to take something from this chapter and use it as part of a dialogue with colleagues, young people and parents about relationships between home and school.

REFERENCES

Askew, S. and Carnell, E. (1996) *School, Home and Professional Networks*, Bristol: Avec.

Athey, C. (1990) *Extending Thought in Young Children*, London: Paul Chapman Publishing.

Bastiani, J. (ed.) (1988) *Parents and Teachers 2: policy to practice*, Windsor: NFER-Nelson.

Clark, A. and Power, S. (1998) *Could Do Better: School Reports and Parents Evenings. A Study of Secondary School Practice*, London: RISE

Crozier, G. (1998) 'Parents and schools: partnership or surveillance?', *Journal of Education Policy* 13:1, 125–136.

Horne, H. (1999) 'Let the sun go down on parents' evenings', *Times*

Educational Supplement, 5 February.

Johnson, D. and Ransom, E. (1983) *Family and School*, London: Croom Helm.

Keogh, J. (1996) 'Governmentality in parent-teacher communications', *Language and Education* 10:2/3, 119–131.

MacBeth, A. (1989) *Involving Parents: effective parent–teacher relations*, Oxford: Heinemann Educational.

Marland, M. (1983) 'Parenting, schooling and mutual learning: a teacher's viewpoint', in J. Bastiani (ed.) (1988) *Parents and Teachers 2: policy to practice*, Windsor: NFER-Nelson

Tizard, B. and Hughes, M. (1984) *Young Children Learning, Talking and Thinking at Home and at School*, London: Collins.

Tizard, B., Blatchford, P., Burke, J., Farquhar, C. and Plewiss, I. (1988) *Young Children at School in the Inner City*, London: Lawrence Erlbaum.

Todd, E. S. and Higgins, S. (1998) 'Powerlessness in professional and parent partnerships', *British Journal of Sociology of Education* 19:2, 227–236.

UNESCO (1996) 'Learning: the treasure within', Report to UNESCO of the International Commission on Education for the 21st Century, Paris: UNESCO.

Walker, B. (1998) 'Meetings without communication: a study of parents' evenings in secondary schools', *British Educational Research Journal* 24:2, 163–178.

Walker, B. and MacLure, M. (1999) *Secondary School Parents' Evenings: a qualitative study*, Norwich: University of East Anglia School of Professional Development.

Wolfendale, S. (1992) *Empowering Parents and Teachers: working for children*, London: Cassell.

Part 3

Feedback for organisational learning

9 Promoting organisational learning in schools – the role of feedback

Jane Reed and Louise Stoll

INTRODUCTION

Schools are in business to promote learning; amongst both adults and pupils. But do they as organisations learn? Is it in fact possible for an organisation as a whole to learn? Even if there is evidence that individuals within organisations are learning, this does not automatically add up to collective learning:

> There are many cases in which organisations know less than their members. There are even cases in which the organisations cannot seem to learn what every member knows.
>
> (Argyris and Schön 1978: 9)

How schools learn to implement complex and multiple change successfully has always been of central concern to those interested in school improvement: making the link between organisational learning and school improvement is not a new idea. Roland Barth claims that school improvement's main task is all about learning:

> School improvement is an effort to determine and provide, from without and within, conditions under which the adults and youngsters who inhabit schools will promote and sustain learning among themselves.
>
> (Barth 1990: 45)

In England especially, schools are under pressure to accommodate and manage change and are constantly dealing with public scrutiny of their effectiveness. Issues they are required to deal with include: a revised National Curriculum, performance management, revised criteria for OFSTED inspections, school self-evaluation, standards for headteachers and subject leaders, as well as the ongoing requirement to improve attainment for all pupils.

In this chapter, we argue that all the activities that constitute learning are a fundamental contribution not just to improvement and performance, but also to an ethos and spirit of community in a school. We outline the importance of organisational learning to school improvement, and highlight the role of feedback, suggesting ways in which its role could be developed. The five questions we ask are:

1   What is organisational learning?
2   Why is it important to school improvement?
3   What are the processes that influence organisational learning?
4   What is the contribution of feedback?
5   How could its role in organisational learning be enhanced?

WHAT IS ORGANISATIONAL LEARNING?

A definition of a learning organisation as it relates to education is:

> a group of people pursuing common purposes (and individual purposes as well) with a collective commitment to regularly weighing the value of those purposes, modifying them when that makes sense, and continuously developing more effective and efficient ways of accomplishing those purposes.
>
> (Leithwood and Aitken 1995: 41)

This definition suggests certain basic activities need to happen for organisational learning to be able to occur:

• the pursuit, review and modification of common aims; and
• opportunities to identify, articulate and design more effective, efficient ways of accomplishing these purposes.

It can be easy for a school to lose sight of its primary purpose of fostering and encouraging learning, particularly in times of increased complexity and requirement to respond to external demands for improvement. As a recent participant on one of our courses put it: 'the core beliefs and goals about learning in my school . . . have been forgotten in the mass of pressures we are under at the moment'.

School improvement research distinguishes more effective and more rapidly improving schools by the ability of practitioners to stay in touch with the school's core values, beliefs and goals and take charge of externally driven change rather than being controlled by it (Senge 1990; Rosenholtz 1991; Stoll and Fink 1996; Gray *et al.* 1999). This is, in Senge's words, because they are constantly enhancing their capacity to create their own future and know that it is in their hands. This mind-set is a cornerstone of effective improvement efforts.

Organisational learning has been described as 'a dynamic and complex phenomenon best understood by considering learning processes and effects as influencing each other in a reciprocal way' (Cousins 1998: 220–1). Through collective inquiry, school staff and their communities engage in processing of internal or external information that challenges them to reflect on and adapt assumptions underpinning their practice. It also helps them to understand how they can influence their own destiny and create the necessary knowledge. In this sense, the basic meaning of a learning organisation is one that is 'continually expanding its capacity to create its future' (Senge 1990: 14).

WHAT ARE THE PROCESSES THAT INFLUENCE ORGANISATIONAL LEARNING?

Our own work suggests four particular processes that can crucially influence the organisational learning of schools. Where these can be deliberately and strategically developed, this facilitates the appropriate conditions and climate within which school improvement can operate. These four processes are: working actively with the context; processing, creating and using strategic knowledge; developing learning-oriented cultural norms; and systems thinking.

Working actively with the context

The articulation of goals that are shared by all stakeholders in a school, including pupils, is not enough in a rapidly changing and demanding context. More than twenty years ago, Argyris and Schön (1978) argued that the key challenge is not to help an organisation become more effective at performing a stable task in the light of stable purposes, but to help an organisation 'restructure its purposes and redefine its task in the face of a changing environment' (p. 320). To do this, schools need to connect more effectively with the world beyond them:

Schools cannot shut their gates and leave the outside world on the doorstep, they can no longer pretend that their walls will keep the outside world at bay.

(Hargreaves and Fullan 1998: 7)

Being able to read the context is a critical skill in effective school improvement. Schools, as other systems, 'must have the capacity to sense, monitor and scan significant aspects of their environment' (Morgan 1996: 87). Intelligent schools know their survival can depend on their sensitive response and adaptation to the environment of which they are a part. This 'contextual intelligence' has been defined as one of nine key intelligences a school needs to have (MacGilchrist *et al.* 1997).

Working to develop and adapt school goals in the light of contextual messages is a crucial purpose for the organisational learning that schools continually need to address. Currently, insufficient notice is being paid to the limited opportunity and power schools feel they have to attend to this basic process. Indeed, the predominant emphasis on the delivery of the external reform agenda paradoxically distracts many schools from initiating their own learning and this results in a loss of both collective self-esteem and of feeling in charge of change (Learmonth and Reed 2000).

Processing, creating and using strategic knowledge

The importance of strategic thinking, planning and action in school improvement together constitute a particular knowledge base required for organisational learning. Louis (1998) argues that what distinguishes organisational learning processes from the notion of acquisition, storage and retrieval inherent in some definitions of individual learning, is an additional step of collective knowledge creation:

Schools cannot learn until there is explicit or implicit agreement about what they know – about their students, teaching and learning, and about how to change.

(p. 1086)

She describes three sources from which this knowledge is drawn: teachers' individual knowledge about the curriculum and their own pedagogical practice; knowledge created when their practice is systematically examined; and knowledge that comes from others, advisers, colleagues, inspectors. Through a combination of dialogue and deliberation, this information is explored, interpreted and distributed among the school community creating collective knowledge and helping powerful learning systems in a school to develop. The process is complex but can also increase the potential for organisational learning in a range of ways. Five assertions have recently been made about the contribution that a strategic approach can make to school improvement (Reed 2000). These are:

1   A strategic approach is underpinned by an explicit commitment to fundamental values and goals in a school.
2   A strategic approach is not just about putting a particular plan into operation. It is a way of working with different levels, goals and expectations at the same time.
3   A strategic approach involves a complex combination of skills – thinking, planning, doing, analysing, judging, reflecting and giving and receiving feedback.
4   A strategic approach is more than a way of achieving coherence. It is a social process that needs to take account of how those involved are feeling and experiencing life in a school as well as supporting them in investing in their own learning.
5   A strategic approach builds knowledge and interest about what is happening as it goes along so that everyone can learn about the process and work together to achieve the agreed goals.

Developing learning-oriented cultural norms

Once schools have identified key aspects of their environment, they must be able to relate this information to the operating norms that guide their current behaviour. Norms are the unspoken rules for what is regarded as customary or acceptable behaviour and action within the school. They are also a window into the deeply held beliefs and values of the school: its culture (Stoll 1999). Leithwood, Jantzi and Steinbach (1998) found that school culture appeared to be the dominant influence on collective learning, more so than vision and mission, structure, strategies, and policy and resources. Rait (1995) explains:

> An organization's culture embodies an informal structure and normative system that influence information flow and other organizational processes. Culture may implicitly or explicitly delineate the boundaries of what is considered proper and improper action.
>
> (p. 83)

Norms are critical because 'Life within a given culture flows smoothly only insofar as one's behaviour conforms with unwritten codes. Disrupt these norms and the ordered reality of life inevitably breaks down' (Morgan 1997: 139). Norms, therefore, shape reactions to internally or externally proposed or imposed improvements and, indeed, to organisational learning. Cultivating learning-oriented norms is, therefore, essential because the acceptance of changes by a school depends on the fit between the norms embedded in the changes and those within the school's own culture (Sarason 1996).

Knowledge needs to have a socially constructed, shared basis for organisational learning to occur (Louis 1994). If norms of individualism and self-reliance exist, and collaboration is not valued, the necessary team learning is at risk. Similarly, schools with norms of contentment, avoidance of change, goal diffusion, top-down leadership, conformity, nostalgia, blame, congeniality rather than collegiality, and denial (Stoll and Fink 1998), are less likely to engage in organisational learning.

Stoll and Fink (1996) identify ten norms that appeared to underpin the work of improving schools: shared goals; responsibility for success; collegiality; continuous improvement; lifelong learning; risk taking; support; mutual respect; openness; celebration and humour. They highlight the human and cultural dimension of change. Two of these merit further discussion for organisational learning.

The first, *collegiality*, involves mutual sharing and assistance, an orientation towards the school as a whole. It is spontaneous, voluntary, development-oriented, unscheduled, and unpredictable. Little (1990) identifies four types of collegial relations. She views three as weaker forms: *scanning and story telling*, general *help and assistance*, and *sharing*. The fourth form, *joint work*, is most likely to lead to improvement and, we would argue, organisational learning. It covers team teaching, mentoring, action research, peer coaching, planning and mutual observation and feedback. These activities create greater interdependence, collective commitment, shared responsibility, and, perhaps most important, 'greater readiness to participate in the difficult business of review and critiques' (Fullan and Hargreaves 1992).

The second norm, *risk taking*, is also critical for organisational learning. Time for experimentation, trial and error and handling failure are essential parts of learning. They symbolise a willingness to try something different, to consider new approaches, and to move into uncharted territory.

The other norms – support, mutual respect, openness, and

celebration and humour – set the important climate that enables risk taking to occur without danger.

Systems thinking

School improvement depends on the use of different 'mental maps' of a school and the creative pursuit of understanding how the whole (the system) and the constituent parts (the subsystems) are relating to each other. Organisational learning occurs where the interdependency of parts and whole, systems and subsystems can be enhanced to enable collective activity to be more effective and satisfying for everyone involved.

Systems thinking has been described as 'a discipline for seeing wholes' (Senge 1990: 68). It is a framework for seeing interrelationships rather than linear cause–effect chains, for seeing patterns and processes of change rather than a static 'snapshot'. The capacity to see patterns and discern connections between seemingly unconnected events emerges as a key feature of organisational learning from both our experience and the literature: 'A systems approach at least helps an investigator understand that the problem is to discover the underlying connections and interdependencies' (Vaill 1996: 108). It is also a crucial tool for improvement efforts, a basis for taking charge of change and feeling more in control. Systems thinking enables a school to analyse more deeply the causal factors that underlie their concerns and difficulties especially where linear deductions of causality fail to get at the root issues. In short, it means it is more important to focus on circles of influence rather than straight lines (Senge 1990). We now take up this point in relation to the role of feedback.

THE NATURE AND CONTRIBUTION OF FEEDBACK IN ORGANISATIONAL LEARNING

One way we have come to understand the contribution of feedback to organisational learning is to take as a starting point Senge's (1990) definition of feedback. He uses the discourse of learning and feedback described as 'loops' in Chapter 1. Feedback as it used here, is different to 'positive feedback' – meaning making encouraging remarks – or 'negative feedback' – meaning potential bad news. It is a broader concept, meaning 'any reciprocal flow of influence' (p. 75) encompassing the notion that every influence is both cause and effect. Indeed, Senge argues that the practice of systems thinking and organisational learning *starts* with understanding feedback. We want to present a view of feedback as an *organisational process that itself can be learned about and used* as well as having the other, more dialogue-based functions that feedback can have in the school community.

O'Connor and McDermott (1997) describe feedback as 'thinking in circles'; hence the notion of feedback loops: the consequences of our actions coming back to us and so influencing what happens next. This concept of feedback challenges immediately any notion that organisational learning can be achieved by either linear or mechanistic means: it needs processing and use of information. Feedback, then, in this sense is the *'return of information* to influence the next step' (O'Connor and McDermott 1997: 26).

Two basic types of feedback loop have been identified. The first is *reinforcing* feedback (Figure 9.1). This describes a situation where change continues to change and grow: a response to something happening makes it happen more frequently. An example from school life could be a response to a high number of exclusions. The school puts in place a procedure for sanctions and rewards, and this results in further exclusions. The feedback from this situation, then, suggests that the procedure for sanctions and rewards itself needs tightening up which, again, unexpectedly causes more exclusions to occur.

The second is *balancing* feedback, which reduces change and restores balance (Figure 9.2). A balancing feedback loop is where the response to something happening makes it happen less (Johnstone 1994: 12–13). An example would be a primary school that on

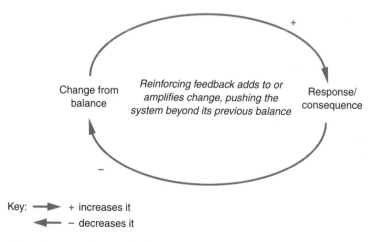

Key: ➤ + increases it
◄─── – decreases it

Figure 9.1 Reinforcing feedback cycle

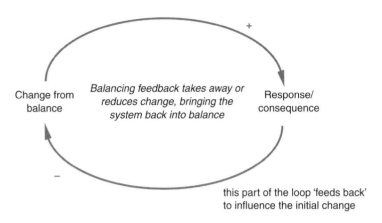

Change from balance

Balancing feedback takes away or reduces change, bringing the system back into balance

Response/ consequence

this part of the loop 'feeds back' to influence the initial change

Figure 9.2 Balancing feedback cycle

analysing its KS1 results finds that the poor quality of spelling is contributing to low attainment. A plan implemented across the Key Stage for addressing spelling more systematically with pupils and their parents enhances their capability, reduces their errors and significantly raises attainment.

Schools as systems are experiencing feedback loops in this way all the time, and to the extent that they are aware of and working with *reinforcing* and *balancing* loops, and are learning how to manage them, they will be in the process of genuinely becoming a learning organisation. Currently, a focus on the analysis of attainment data and making causal links to practice in the classroom can provide good examples of use of feedback. Significant connections are being made from one part of the school (the data) to another (the learning and teaching programme), and in the process organisational learning can occur.

Morgan (1997) and others have reminded us of a key element in organisational learning processes which may influence the direction a reinforcing cycle takes – towards growth or decline. Organisations may display adaptive learning which solves problems at an operational level: they scan the environment, compare against the operating targets, and initiate appropriate action (the single loop learning in Figure 9.3). In so doing, they show the ability to detect and correct deviations from the norm. Many organisations are quite proficient at this including bureaucratic, fragmented organisations where employees are not encouraged to think for themselves and interest in what the organisation is doing is marginal.

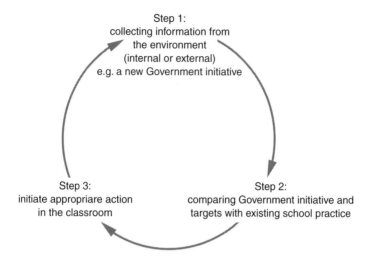

Figure 9.3 Single loop learning

However, single loop learning may keep an organisation focused on the wrong goals and prevent success in a changing environment. Effective organisations require 'double loop learning' (Figure 9.4) in which the crucial extra ingredient is to question whether the operating targets are relevant and whether the norms are appropriate. This is generative learning which solves fundamental problems in a creative way and facilitates survival in periods of change.

Morgan suggests that when people are unable or not prepared to challenge underlying assumptions, 'The existence of single-loop learning systems, especially when used as controls over employees, may prevent double-loop learning from occurring' (1997: 90). The capacity in a school to reflect on its own learning while it is using the information provided by feedback is crucial. Ertmer and Newby (1996) outline the characteristics of an expert learner, which include the capacity to regulate one's own learning, to self-monitor. It is possible to see that this capacity in a school, to use and reflect on feedback processes, is a key capability in a learning organisation.

The following example illustrates the value of questioning while using feedback. A school joined one of our school improvement projects with the view that a group of Key Stage 2 pupils were, in the staff's description, restless and lacking concentration in their lessons because they had poor listening skills. It was to be the focus for their project. These were not pupils with any obvious learning difficulties.

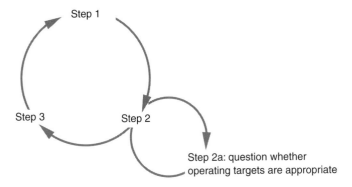

Figure 9.4 Double loop learning

The teachers stated clearly that they wanted to improve the listening skills of these pupils. We cautioned them not to jump to conclusions before they had carried out a careful systemic audit and analysis of the context in which this problem was manifesting itself. They reluctantly agreed. What emerged from the audit was a very different kind of 'causal' picture. The process of gathering information showed that this group were actually very good listeners in settings that sufficiently caught their attention and enabled them to access the curriculum in ways that made sense to them. Through examining the wider system that the pupils were part of, it seemed that this group of pupils were signalling through their lack of engagement that schemes of work and teaching processes were inadequately differentiated for them. Improving this practice was the focus of a very successful project in the school. The teachers learnt to look at their whole situation in a more sophisticated way instead of jumping too quickly to conclusions based in their minds on a linear and more simplistic model of the relationship between learning, teaching and achievement.

The situation these teachers found themselves in is a very good example of reinforcing feedback. The more the pupils had a learning diet that did not meet their needs, the more they did not listen. When the school gave them a more carefully designed programme of activities the listening skills of the pupils were shown to be perfectly satisfactory. The balancing feedback process had produced the results that they wanted and staff had learnt a great deal about those pupils, their needs and most importantly about the impact of their teaching.

HOW CAN THE ROLE OF FEEDBACK IN ORGANISATIONAL LEARNING BE ENHANCED?

We have considered schools' use of feedback in their organisational learning processes, but how can people in schools collectively learn to use feedback to change their practices, solve problems and enhance learning and teaching? Here, we suggest two ways that might offer avenues for further exploration.

More effective ways of presenting feedback

A range of pupil data is currently presented to schools as a basis of feedback for organisational learning and action. It is a very topical pursuit in school improvement in UK schools at the moment. Often data related to pupils' academic results or attitudes arrive in schools on printout sheets or in booklets, sometimes with accompanying diagrams and brief notes of explanation. Interpretation and use of data are now an essential activity for schools, with the aim of improving (amongst other things) teaching and learning programmes. Many schools have been asking for help in understanding and using data about pupils' attainment.

Statistical overload can become an issue as can deciding the important issues to pursue. This can lead to data not being analysed or used – almost a reinforcing feedback cycle of its own, since 'Little frustrates or demoralises teachers more than painstakingly collected information which is apparently unused' (Learmonth and Lowers 1998: 137). In addition, schools can be confused by 'the myth of numbers'. Even value added results, describing pupils' progress, come with confidence intervals, which means it is hard to separate schools reliably to produce fine rankings (Goldstein 1992). This leads to the inaccuracy of some league tables and bench-marked league tables, where schools are compared against those with similar catchment areas.

When feedback is 'delivered', the way this is handled can be mismanaged. It resonates of the discourse of 'gift' outlined in Chapter 1. Lack of participation in analysing and interpreting the feedback that data can give, leads to limited learning. On the other hand, teachers may have clear views on 'the most useful source of help'. Cousins and Leithwood (1993) studied such external 'knowledge utilisation' in improving the primary curriculum. The following qualities of the information source were particularly important:

- *Sophistication* – the perceived quality of the information source, including its technical sophistication, appropriateness and rigour.

- *Credibility* – the perceived believability and validity of the source of help, and those responsible for disseminating it (track record and expertise).
- *Relevance* – the extent to which the audience for whom it was intended perceived the knowledge to be pertinent and practical.
- *Communication quality* – the perceived clarity, style and readability, with which the knowledge was conveyed.
- *Content* – the nature and substance of the actual knowledge being disseminated, especially whether or not the content was perceived to be congruent with existing knowledge, valued, positive and of sufficient scope.
- *Timeliness* – the extent to which knowledge was perceived to be disseminated at an appropriate time and in an ongoing manner.

Effective use of critical friends

Outsiders offering schools critical friendship as a basis for dialogue can be invaluable to developing organisational learning capacity. Schools need an external perspective to observe what is not immediately apparent to those working on the inside. These individuals and groups can watch and listen, ask thought-provoking questions about formal and informal data that help those in schools sort out their thinking, make sound decisions and determine appropriate strategies. This relationship, however, is more likely to work when it is based on trust and support, where critical friends bring an open mind and a commitment to mutual exchange, rather than their own vested interests. Consequently, when the feedback critical friends convey contains difficult messages, these are more likely to be heard and taken on board. A longer-term outcome of effective critical friendship appears to be the ability to help a school become its own critical friend. In considering the role and value of critical friends in twenty-four Scottish primary and secondary schools involved in the Improving School Effectiveness Project (ISEP), MacBeath (1998) notes:

> There is one touchstone question for the critical friend, which is not too far away from what a teacher would, or should, ask in relation to the class or individual learner: 'Will this help to develop independence, the capacity to learn and to apply learning more effectively over time?'
>
> (p. 131)

An example comes from the comments of a primary school headteacher describing the benefits of their critical friend:

He appeared to value each individual situation and what each person had to offer to that situation; you felt at ease in his company. He helped us to keep focused and positive about the situation here. After the initial results the staff morale in the school sank and the staff were zonked. The critical friend quickly brought us back to looking at the positives and look at what we were actually doing and not at what we were not doing He helped us to be reflective, how we could improve our own practice He was not judgemental . . . He respected people's point of view. Much of the development here has come from within the staff. People have not rushed outside for solutions. This is the way the change in development has taken place.

Phases of the critical friend relationship may be distinguished. The early stages are important for establishing ground rules, agreeing broad parameters within which the school and project staff will work, and creating a 'mutual comfort zone' (MacBeath 1998). Developing a spirit of trust appears to be important in enabling people to speak openly and share thoughts, ideas and concerns with others. 'Trust is a Must' if feedback is to be used effectively.

In the next stage, moving out of the 'comfort zone' with senior staff, critical friends need to clarify their neutral role. The ISEP team found that data presentation can be a sensitive task, but the situation can be eased if critical friends are totally familiar with the data and comfortable with handling it and its interpretation, both generally as a research instrument and within the context of the particular school involved. It is important to explain it clearly and unambiguously, leaving no room for confusion. Furthermore, valid interpretation is necessary, to enable schools to see the realities of their own situations objectively. This requires careful listening, reflection on the issues raised, reformulation of interpretations, and picking out positive aspects and encouraging people to reflect on how they can be built on.

A third stage can be characterised by the questions 'where do we go from here and how do we set about it?'. Most notably, this is the time when the critical friend begins to move more from the role of friend to that of critic. Respect for individual confidentiality continues to be important, but so are helping others to self-evaluate; presenting examples from elsewhere in such a way that teachers can reflect on the relative merits of each; challenging people to broaden and extend their self-perception; 'referee' discussions; encouragement; praising, clarifying and revisiting issues to help people maintain momentum; and, where necessary, playing the role of confidant.

In all they do, more effective critical friends are aware they need to leave schools more self-sufficient in their own improvement processes. In moving towards the final stage of disengagement, therefore, the critical friend helps people move to a reflective, dialogic approach that incorporates greater openness to questioning and a respect for evidence: 'The question "how do you know?" eventually ceases to be put by the critical friend and becomes a routine way of thinking' (MacBeath 1998: 129).

CLOSING COMMENT

When new information or knowledge is introduced as a result of feedback, individual members of an organisation process it through their own frame of reference, their particular mental representation of their world.

It is, however, in the process of interaction, dialogue and deliberation about information, that shared representations and understandings for the organisation as a whole occur. This becomes organisational learning when members are able to interpret the new in a way that adds to their collective sense of their core business and how to set about it. Its outcome is hopefully a commitment to being 'inquiry minded' and adaptive to change in the light of their common purposes.

We want to suggest in summary that feedback can have four main functions in organisational learning. Feedback has a *bridging* function when it can link otherwise separate or disparate information and bring these into a useful relationship with each other. Feedback has an *illuminative* function when it sheds light on problems or conundrums that seem otherwise insoluble and enables a school to move forward. Feedback has a *challenging* function when it enables the reframing of information in a way that brings new meaning to bear. Feedback can *renew purpose* when it re-connects a school to its primary task of educating young people and is reminded that they are the primary motivation for all organisational learning.

REFERENCES

Argyris, C. and Schön, D. A. (1978) *Organizational Learning: a theory of action perspective*, Reading MA: Addison-Wesley.

Barth, R. (1990) *Improving Schools from Within: teachers, parents and principals can make the difference*, San Francisco: Jossey-Bass.

Cousins, J. B. (1998) 'Intellectual roots of organizational learning', in K. Leithwood and K. S. Louis (eds) *Organizational Learning in Schools*, Lisse: Swets and Zeitlinger.

Cousins, J. B. and Leithwood, K. (1993) 'Enhancing knowledge utilization as a strategy for school improvement', *Knowledge: Creation, Diffusion, Utilization* 14: 3, 305–333.

Ertmer P. A. and Newby T. J. (1996) 'The expert learner: strategic, self regulated and reflective', *Instructional Science* 24: 1, 1–24.

Fullan, M. and Hargreaves, A. (1992) *What's Worth Fighting for in Your School?*, Buckingham: Open University Press.

Goldstein H. (1992) 'Editorial: statistical information and the measurement of education outcomes', *Journal of the Royal Statistical Society A* 155:3, 313–315.

Gray, J., Hopkins, D., Reynolds, D., Wilcox, B., Farrell, S. and Jesson, D. (1999) *Improving Schools: performance and potential*, Buckingham: Open University Press.

Hargreaves, A. and Fullan, M. (1998) *What's Worth Fighting for in Education?*, Buckingham: Open University Press.

Johnstone, C. (1994) *The Lens of Deep Ecology*, London: IDEE.

Learmonth, J. and Lowers, K. (1998) 'A trouble shooter calls: the role of the independent consultant', in L. Stoll and K. Myers (eds) *No Quick Fixes: perspectives on schools in difficulty*, London: Falmer Press.

Learmonth, J. and Reed, J. (2000) 'Revitalising Teachers' Accountability: learning about learning as a renewed focus for school improvement', paper presented at the Thirteenth International Congress for School Effectiveness and Improvement, Hong Kong, January.

Leithwood, K. and Aitken, R. (1995) *Making Schools Smarter*, Thousand Oaks CA: Corwin.

Leithwood, K. and Louis, K.S. (eds) (1998) *Organizational Learning in Schools*, Lisse: Swets and Zeitlinger.

Leithwood, K., Jantzi, D. and Steinbach, R. (1998) 'Leadership and other conditions which foster organizational learning in schools', in K. Leithwood and K. S. Louis (eds) *Organizational Learning in Schools*, Lisse: Swets and Zeitlinger.

Little, J. W. (1990) 'The persistence of privacy: autonomy and initiative in teachers professional relations', *Teachers College Record* 91:4, 509–536.

Louis, K. S. (1994) 'Beyond managed change', *School Effectiveness and School Improvement* 5:1, 2–25.

Louis, K. S. (1998) 'Reconnecting knowledge utilization and school improvement', in A. Hargreaves, A. Lieberman, M. Fullan and D. Hopkins (eds) *International Handbook of Educational Change. Part 2*, Dordrecht: Kluwer.

MacBeath, J. (1998) 'I didn't know he was ill: the role and value of the critical friend', in L. Stoll and K. Myers (eds) *No Quick Fixes: perspectives on schools in difficulty* London: Falmer Press.

MacGilchrist, B., Myers, K. and Reed, J. (1997) *The Intelligent School*, London: Paul Chapman.

Morgan, G. (1996) *Images of Organizations*, Newbury Park, CA: Sage.

Morgan, G. (1997) *Images of Organization* (2nd edn), London: Sage.

O'Connor, J. and McDermott, I. (1997) *The Art of Systems Thinking*, London: Thorsons.

Rait, E. (1995) 'Against the current: organizational learning in schools', in S. B. Bacharach and B. Mundell (eds) *Images of Schools: structures and roles in organizational behavior*, London: Sage.

Reed J. E. (2000) 'Strategic thinking in the Malawi school support system project', unpublished materials developed for Ministry of Education, Malawi.

Rosenholtz, S. J. (1991) *Teachers' Workplace: the social organization of schools*, New York: Longman

Sarason, S. B. (1996) *Revisiting 'The Culture of the School and the Problem of Change'*, New York: Teachers College Press.

Senge, P. M. (1990) *The Fifth Discipline: the art and practice of the learning organisation*, London: Century Business.

Stoll, L. (1999) 'School culture: black hole or fertile garden for improvement', in J. Prosser (ed.) *School Culture*, London: Paul Chapman.

Stoll, L. A. and Fink, D. (1996) *Changing Our Schools: linking school effectiveness and school improvement*, Buckingham: Open University Press.

Stoll, L. and Fink, D. (1998) 'The cruising school: the unidentified ineffective school', in L. Stoll and K. Myers (eds) *No Quick Fixes: perspectives on schools in difficulty*, London: Falmer Press.

Stoll, L., MacBeath, J., Smith, I. and Robertson, P. (forthcoming) 'The change equation: capacity for improvement, in improving school effectiveness', in J. MacBeath and P. Mortimore (eds) *Improving School Effectiveness*, Buckingham: Open University Press.

Vaill, P. B. (1996) *Learning As a Way of Being: strategies for survival in a world of permanent white water*, San Francisco: Jossey-Bass.

10 Value added feedback for the purpose of school self-evaluation

Sally Thomas, Rebecca Smees and Karen Elliot

INTRODUCTION

> Of course, information about performance cannot raise standards on its own. It is the uses to which such information is put that are vital.
>
> (Mortimore 1998: 218)

School and teacher self-evaluation has always played a part in the development of educational standards and practices, in addition to external evaluations carried out, for example, by HMI. However, in the last ten years or so the accumulation of evidence on schools' effectiveness and improvement has focused the attention of policy makers on the possibilities for improving educational practice, pupil performance and overall standards. This has resulted in policies requiring more systematic approaches to school and teacher evaluation – both internal and external. Teachers are now encouraged to use performance data provided by the DfEE, as well as other evidence, to inform their own evaluations of the education they provide (DfEE 1998a). This approach involves an on-going and systematic self-evaluation of teacher's educational practices and improvement processes using both quantitative and qualitative information drawn from a variety of sources. Local Education Authorities (LEAs) in England also now have a statutory role in monitoring the quality of education and improvements in all schools in their region. At the national level, OFSTED inspection reports and school league tables of raw examination results continue to be published as a mechanism for external evaluation and accountability.

In the context of these policy developments this chapter aims to focus specifically on one particular aspect of school evaluations: the methodology, uses and limitations of value added feedback for the purpose of school and teacher self-evaluation. We will draw on recent findings from our work on value added measures of schools' effectiveness and will also contrast the findings with examples of how secondary schools in Lancashire use value added and other feedback data to inform their educational practices.

WHAT IS VALUE ADDED FEEDBACK?

In education, the term 'value added' has been used in recent years as a general indicator of quality but also as a specific way of conceptualising and measuring school effectiveness (Saunders 1998). In the latter case, the value added concept is based on the idea of measuring the progress of students in a particular school *relative* to the progress made by students in other schools during a given period of time. Usually progress is defined in terms of academic or cognitive outcomes such as reading or mathematics. However, the value added concept can also be applied to non-cognitive outcomes such as students' attitudes (on a Likert type scale) or measures of vocational competence (Thomas 1998).

In order to measure *relative* progress baseline and outcome measures are required at the beginning and end of a particular time period (for example, covering all or part of the primary or secondary phases of education) for a large and representative sample of schools (at least forty). During children's time at school one would expect them to make some progress or improvement and therefore average attainment levels to rise. Thus 'value added' feedback refers to measures of the extra boost that is added by schools to pupil attainment over and above the progress or improvement that might be expected in a normative sense. For the purpose of internal school self-evaluation, value added feedback aims to provide teachers with meaningful, valid and accurate measures of the progress of their own students relative to students in other schools. The objective is that this evidence, alongside other measures of a school's quality and processes, can be used by teachers to inform, reflect on and learn about their professional and educational practice. Moreover, if practitioners are willing to share their reflections and learning then this process may assist in identifying best practice and successful innovations in teaching and learning. Examples of this approach are provided by a case study of one Lancashire school later in the chapter.

MEASURING VALUE ADDED

Measuring the effect a school has on student progress is complex. In part this is because the educational experiences of any individual student, and the wide variety of factors influencing her or his progress, can be viewed as unique and almost impossible to quantify. However, the more information it is possible to have about individual students, subgroups of students, and all students in a school as well as comparative data across a whole population (or representative sample) of schools, the more reliable and informative any subsequent analysis is likely to be. As mentioned previously, the key evidence required to measure a student's relative progress is baseline and outcome attainment data over a specific period of time. The statistical methodology of calculating value added scores is well established and described in detail elsewhere (Goldstein 1997). However, essentially value added measures reflect the extent to which students are performing above or below the level expected on the basis of their previous attainments and are calculated in terms of standard assessment units (e.g. GCSE point score, National Curriculum levels).

Employing purely outcome and prior attainment data is one straightforward approach to measuring students' relative progress which does not have in-built assumptions about the possible impact of any external factors influencing student progress. However, to provide a more fine tuned measure additional background and contextual information about individual students and schools may also be needed. It is important to acknowledge at this point that it is impossible to provide statistical adjustment for *all* factors outside the control of the school which have a significant impact on student performance. Therefore we should emphasise that value added feedback represents the school effect *and other effects not accounted for in the analysis.*

DIFFERENT TYPES OF VALUE ADDED FEEDBACK

We now turn to the issue of how value added feedback measures reflect the complex nature of school effectiveness. A recent ESRC-funded study carried out by Thomas and Smees shows that to provide a realistic picture of a school's performance a range of different value added measures is required to reveal the internal variations in school effectiveness across one or more dimensions. These dimensions include student outcomes in different aspects of the curriculum, different cohorts, different curriculum stages and different student groups (Thomas 1999).

Different aspects of the curriculum

Previous evidence shows that in some cases school effects can vary quite substantially between different academic subject outcomes (e.g. English, mathematics, science) and indicates that schools can have quite different effects in different subject areas or departments (Thomas *et al.* 1997). Interestingly, across different regions the consistency of secondary schools departmental effectiveness can vary suggesting that whole school policies may have a greater impact in some regions (e.g. Lancashire) than in others (e.g. London) (Thomas 1999).

In addition to the results between academic outcomes, our work has shown the relationship between schools' value added scores for academic and student attitude measures is relatively weak (Thomas *et al.* 2000). Educationally important, these new findings support earlier work at the primary level (Mortimore *et al.* 1988) and tentatively suggest that separate dimensions of effectiveness can be identified for different aspects of how schools and teachers can influence pupils' attitudes and achievements.

This evidence strongly suggests the need to examine school effectiveness measures across a range of academic outcomes in order to reveal the pattern of departmental or subject area performance. Clearly, using a single measure effectiveness may conceal important within school differences not only across academic aspects of the curriculum but also other aspects such as vocational or attitudinal outcomes (Scheerens and Bosker 1997).

Different cohorts

The importance of examining trends in school effects over time (i.e. value added scores for consecutive student cohorts) is clear. This is because 'real' improvement (or decline) in performance, resulting perhaps from a shift in educational policy or practice, can only be identified by examining long-term changes in results over time. Indeed, the educational processes associated with particular patterns of improvement have recently been reported by Gray *et al.* (1999).

However, Thomas and Smees have found that the stability or instability of school value added results for individual cohorts varied depending on which analysis method was employed. Therefore, different methods are appropriate according to the intended purpose and use of the results. Using a separate analysis for each cohort emphasises instability over time and this method is appropriate for the purpose of examining in detail the improvement (or decline) in value added scores for individual cohorts from year to year. In contrast value added results that are measured in terms of linear trends or a kind of 'rolling average' of two or more consecutive cohorts are more stable over time. This kind of feedback is appropriate to examine long-term patterns of school performance.

To demonstrate these two approaches we have employed the 1993–1997 GCSE data from Lancashire LEA to produce two contrasting plots showing the total GCSE score[2] results from a separate value added analysis for each cohort (Figure 10.1) and the equivalent results using 'rolling averages' where each value added measure includes three consecutive GCSE cohorts (Figure 10.2). On each plot a single time trend line for each school is shown for a random sub-sample Lancashire secondary schools. Interestingly, the time trend lines for most schools in Figure 10.2 appear to be nearly parallel, thus indicating that few schools have changed substantially in their value added performance over the five-year period. Indeed, the Thomas and Smees findings show that differences between schools in value added time trends are either not statistically significant or much smaller than previously reported by Gray *et al.* (1996). Moreover, the range in schools' effectiveness – as measured by their value added scores – appears to be

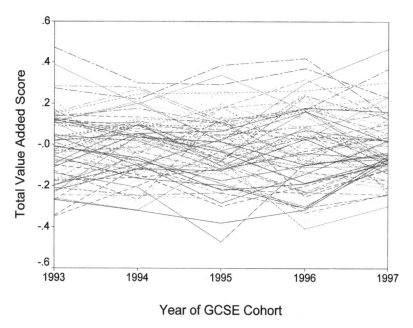

Year of GCSE Cohort

Figure 10.1 Total GCSE Value Added Scores from individual year analyses

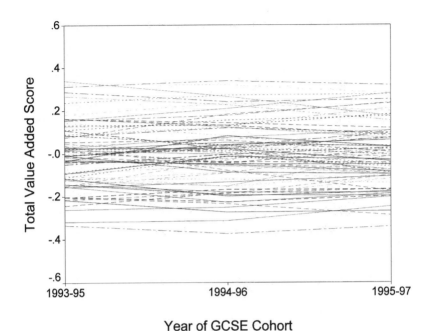

Year of GCSE Cohort

Figure 10.2 Total GCSE Value Added Scores from combined three year analyses

fairly constant over time. A key question for future research is whether improvements in raw GCSE results can be achieved by all schools to the extent that differences in schools' effectiveness decline. Alternatively, if raw GCSE score improvements can only be maintained by some schools and not by others, then there is a real possibility that differences in schools' effectiveness may eventually appear to increase.

These results have an important message for government policy makers, as well as teachers and researchers. That is, irrespective of many schools' apparent improvement in raw league table performance, only a small minority have been able to improve substantially in their effectiveness – *relative to that of other schools*.

Different curriculum stages

The Thomas and Smees study also presents new and previously unreported findings about schools' effects for Key Stage 3 and Key Stages 3 and 4 combined by using 1997 data from Lancashire. The results show that some schools can obtain quite different value added scores according to whether the whole or only part of the secondary curriculum is examined and suggest the existence of separate effectiveness dimensions for different National Curriculum stages. For government policy makers these findings are particularly relevant given the publication (DfEE 1998b) of a sample of schools' value added results for Key Stage 4 only. In the light of the current findings a school could appear to be doing well at Key Stage 4, but not so well at Key Stage 3 or across both Key Stages 3 and 4. Overall the results indicate that separate value added measures of effectiveness should be fed back to schools for each Key Stage as well as for the whole period of secondary schooling.

Different student groups

Value added research in the last ten years has examined the issue of differential school and departmental effects for different groups of students (such as high and low attainers, boys and girls or different ethnic groups) and found that an important aspect of a school's effectiveness was whether it was equally effective for *all* student groups. By employing detailed student level data and controlling for previous attainment and other background factors the evidence shows that using an overall measure of school (or departmental) performance may mask important differences in the relative progress made by different student groups, particularly those categorised by prior attainment and entitlement to free school meals (FSM – a measure of disadvantage). Interestingly, the consistency of school and departmental effects for different pupil groups categorised by prior attainment appears to be stronger in some regions (e.g. the Netherlands) than in others (e.g. London) and may be due to regional differences in the extent of pupil selection. However, we would argue that further research is required to clarify this issue (Thomas 1999).

To examine the FSM differential results in more detail the Thomas and Smees study carried out an analysis using a value added measure which includes only prior attainment explanatory variables and therefore does not make the assumption that average attainment differences exist between particular groups. Using this approach, for example in Lancashire over the period 1993–1997, only 22 per cent of schools obtained positive value added scores for pupils entitled to FSM, whereas 72 per cent of schools obtained positive scores for non-FSM pupils. Moreover, in 93 per cent of schools FSM pupils make less progress on average than other pupils. In spite of the crudeness of the

FSM indicator, these findings could be usefully interpreted as schools having different levels of effectiveness for pupils who are more (or less) advantaged economically and have important implications about pupil entitlement within schools. Crucially, a minority of schools did appear to narrow the attainment gap between disadvantaged and other pupils suggesting that some educational practices can be successful in addressing under-achievement. For the purpose of self-evaluation and monitoring equal opportunities this evidence points to schools' need for fine-tuned value added feedback (controlling for both prior attainment and other factors such as disadvantage) but, in addition, comparative feedback that makes explicit the absolute levels of *progress* made by different pupil groups.

INTERPRETING VALUE ADDED FEEDBACK

Regional differences and effectiveness at other levels of the education system

Evidence of regional or national differences in the size of school effects is vital to inform teachers and policy makers about the influence of local area, regional and national policy and practice on pupil performance. Findings by Thomas and Smees show that regional differences do appear to exist in terms of the size and impact of school effects, and these are mirrored by differences in regional context. This evidence points to the *interpretation* of school effects being regionally dependent and therefore highlights the need for teachers and policy makers to take into account the regional or policy context when evaluating school performance.

We would argue that effectiveness at different levels of the education system (e.g. individual pupils, classrooms, departments, whole school, LEA, region and nationally) as well as interactions between levels need to be continually monitored in order to inform the development of policy and practice and map out the *boundaries* of school effectiveness. In addition, teachers may usefully employ value added data at the pupil and class level in order to identify any unusual pattern of results within their school and the possible explanation for any outliers observed.

Limitations of value added feedback

So far we have outlined the importance of providing effectiveness indicators in a range of different dimensions or areas. However, when trying to make sense of value added measures it is crucial to emphasise the statistical significance or uncertainty of any numerical data so as to avoid misinterpretation of the results. By the term *'statistical uncertainty'* we mean the uncertainty involved in estimating any average numerical score from a sample of observations, scores or measurements. This uncertainty prevents any fine distinctions being made between the performance of most schools, departments or classrooms (Goldstein 1997). It is also important to consider the issue of *measurement error* when interpreting data based on measures of student attainment. *Measurement error* is the error associated with trying to obtain a 'true' measure of an individual student's attainment from an 'observed' measure of their attainment at one specific point in time.

Thus, the value of school effectiveness measures is defined to a large extent, by the quality, reliability and validity of the data analysed. Another issue which is difficult to address is the accuracy and appropriateness of the data. For example, the indicator of student disadvantage 'eligible for free schools meals' (FSM) may be inaccurate because some parents do not apply for an eligibility means test. Furthermore, the system does not cover completely all students likely to suffer from social and economic disadvantage. Other relevant measures of socio-economic status, such as level of parental education, occupation and income are difficult and costly to collect. Nevertheless, FSM is currently the most readily available, easily updated measure of socio-economic disadvantage among school children.

The limitations of value added (and other) measures should be realistically addressed as an important part of school self-evaluation activities. In practice this means always considering the statistical significance of individual school results, and also where possible the stability of results over time, as well as other relevant data or evidence of a school's quality or processes that may be available in a school. In addition, the retrospective nature of the data needs to be well understood. Value added feedback is a valid and useful tool for reflecting on past performance and practices, to raise questions and to point to the need for further evidence (Elliot *et al.* 1998). However, if the data are used as an indicator of future performance then there is a real danger that previous patterns will be continually repeated. It is important to recognise that *all* pupils can potentially achieve at the highest level and therefore past performance does not necessarily predict future performance. This issue is demonstrated by the existence of schools where all pupils perform well irrespective of their previous attainments or background.

USING VALUE ADDED RESULTS FOR SCHOOL
SELF-EVALUATION

We have emphasised the need for schools to analyse data in a more sensitive and detailed way, at a range of levels. However, in order to implement a value added system of school self-evaluation it is important that schools are willing to collaborate with other schools at the local, regional and national level in order to provide comparative data. In the following section we provide an overview of the Lancashire LEA value added project and summarise the findings of a case study of self-evaluation activities in one school to provide examples of how teachers can use value added data to inform their practice.

LANCASHIRE LEA VALUE ADDED PROJECT

The Lancashire value added project was set up in 1992 and aims to provide an innovative system of secondary school evaluation and self-evaluation via the feedback of student outcome and performance data (Thomas and Mortimore 1996). This information is intended to inform the improvement processes of state-funded schools within the Lancashire LEA region. The evaluation process is not intended for external accountability purposes, rather, as a tool for internal accountability and school improvement, in terms of assessing the performance of different subjects and groups of pupils as well as the whole school. The LEA tries extremely hard to encourage schools to use the value added data confidentially for 'internal purposes only', not to disclose such information to parents or the press, to prevent any of the negative aspects of the raw league tables:

> A key element within it [the project] has been the integrity of the data because what we have never wanted to do is to publish an alternative league table. (LEA adviser and project manager)

Since the early beginnings, the project has expanded to incorporate a number of different types of value added and other feedback generated from the London Institute of Education and the LEA, as well as agencies such as the National Consortium of Examination Results. For example, the London Institute now provides a total of forty-four different GCSE value added measures as well as comparative feedback on pupils' attitudes (Smees and Thomas 1998; Thomas 1998; Thomas *et al.* 2000). In addition, some individual schools have developed customised ways of presenting and using the results via graphical feedback, predicted grades, school-specific questionnaires and attendance data. LEA support in the process of using the value added scores is ongoing. A series of LEA seminars on value added are held for schools every year, as well as separate sessions for school governors. However, Lancashire schools are still in the process of learning in terms of self-evaluation activities, and although a lot of the schools use the data, there is a small minority that do not understand fully what the scores mean. The LEA project manager reported:

> the vast majority of schools can have an intelligent conversation on this data now. (LEA adviser and project manager)

The introduction of value added scores for different ability bands has led to closer attention to the differing needs of different pupil groups within the school. Many schools have adopted able pupil policies, streaming of pupils, and changes in the curriculum to fit with the different ability groups. The profile of systematic individual pupil monitoring has also increased as a consequence of the project. Assessment systems, setting targets for pupils, and whole school approaches such as calling in school books have been set up to:

> monitor progress and attainment, to monitor the way in which the assessment of pupils is being carried out and how that assessment information is being used to plan future learning strategies for individual improvement. (LEA adviser and project manager)

The project also seems to be having an effect on schools reflecting on the quality of teaching and learning within the school. Advisers are working with heads of department, heads of faculty and senior managers to look at strategies to develop monitoring of teaching and learning quality, an application that the LEA hope to develop much more in the future, when they hope to network similar departments with differing attainment success:

> It's all about opening up schools for a much more detailed and critical analysis about what is the best practice we can find, what is it that is successful and how can we actually improve and disseminate improvement strategies and ideas. (LEA adviser and project manager)

In terms of evaluating improvement, schools use both the value added and raw GCSE results to carefully examine trends in pupils academic performance over the seven years of the project. The '*3 year rolling average*' results are a particularly useful aid to valid interpretations of improvement as year-to-year fluctuations in results are smoothed out. Schools have also employed the pupil questionnaire results related to different aspects of school culture, such as bullying and behaviour, to investigate the impact of current policy and practice as well as new initiatives:

> Things like anti-bullying policies, behaviour policy, they love things like that [i.e. as reflected in the questionnaire item results] to see whether or not they have got that right in the school. (LEA adviser and project manager)

In terms of the current national policy of setting pupil attainment targets for each school and the LEA, the Lancashire Value Added Project feeds into the whole process by enabling fairer school targets to be set:

> What we are able to do is to take into account measures of prior attainment, we are able to take into account trends when all background factors using multilevel analysis, take those factors into account and as a result of that start to set quite reasonable targets for schools. (LEA adviser and project manager)

A CASE STUDY OF SELF-EVALUATION ACTIVITIES IN ONE LANCASHIRE SECONDARY SCHOOL

To provide an illustration of school self-evaluation activities we have drawn on evidence from a case study of one Lancashire secondary school. The case study school was selected, with the advice of LEA managers, on the basis of illustrating good practice in school self-evaluation activities. Interviews were recorded over a two-day period and involved separate interviews with the head teacher, deputy heads, heads of department, classroom teachers, pupils, parents and governors. In terms of context the school has recently become a Technology College and is situated within a mixed economic setting of state-funded council housing accommodation and middle-class suburbs.

The Lancashire Value Added Project feeds into the school's own self-evaluation programme and this was originally conceptualised as a tool to facilitate the turn-around of the school. Evaluation data helped

the school to understand the problems they faced, and most importantly, to begin to grapple with issues in a completely new way. It was
this self-empowerment that was the major push towards improvement:

> I think it was really fairly quickly that we began to realise what a
> powerful tool that we had got. For first of all, I suppose selfishly,
> I was their head and for me as a management tool it was the one
> thing I would never give up, because it has enabled me to under-
> stand so many things better than I have understood before, and to
> deal with them, I think, in a more dynamic and positive way.
> (Headteacher)

However, the programme did not materialise overnight, and it was
soon realised that the initial work they had embarked on, looking at
the results of previous cohorts of pupils, although useful to the school,
did not directly help the pupils presently attending. This led in time to
the reconceptualisation of the programme within the school to include
systematic individual monitoring of all pupils as part of the self-
evaluation process, via predicted grades, on-going assessments and the
use of interim reports. The pupil level evaluation data also influence the
planning of classroom practices. The data they have on entry year
attainment allow the teachers to tailor the teaching approach to the
particular children they have in the class:

> Well, I would make decisions about the kind of work that I am
> doing and the way I'm going about revision with the KS4 class
> based on what I know of them. (Department Head)

Such data also give the teachers a guide to the reasons a child might
not be achieving, leading to different teaching strategies for different
pupils within the class. Such knowledge can help teachers manage the
classroom more effectively, and enable them to keep a closer eye on
pupils who may need more intensive help.

Evaluation of whole school and departmental results is also an integral part of the self-evaluation programme. Information from the Value
Added Project produced by the LEA and the London Institute of
Education is discussed and assessed in individual meetings between
heads of faculty, head and deputy head. However, most staff at the
school are very much focused on the pupils in their own classes and
looking internally for answers, rather than outside the school. They felt
the school, any school and each class within it is unique, so the best
place to begin looking for solutions is within the school itself. Part of

the coming year's agenda is for the heads of faculty to look at how they can 'pick out' best practice from the different departments in the coming year, which would work alongside the existing system of classroom observation. At present each teacher is allowed covered time each term to observe a class of their choice, often pairing with either a highly effective subject or one closely related to their own. This helps towards dissemination of best practice:

> We are all doing little bits of a good job but if you can sort of mould that and pick out the best bits and all do that, then that would give overall exam success. (Department Head)

Teachers are clearly willing to take responsibility for the welfare of their own students and their performance. As one teacher asked:

> How I can make a difference? How can I put things right if I've made a mistake or done something wrong? (Class teacher)

Interestingly staff interviewed recognised a concern that the outcomes measured within education concentrate heavily on academic outcomes, at the expense of other equally valuable educational indicators:

> There are so many other things that are not easily measurable that we know we do because we work here, we live here, we know the children and only people in the school can do that. You can't always measure it, it comes from experience, it comes from feelings. (Deputy Head and project manager)

A SUMMARY OF GOOD PRACTICE

The selected case study school illustrates current good practice in self-evaluation activities where evaluation data are incorporated into all levels of school practice from classroom teaching to staff appraisal. The following self-evaluation strategies seem to be particularly effective:

- An intensive monitoring system, that tracks students throughout their school career, and has within it a programme of intervention if students are falling behind.
- A clear, shared focus on high expectations for all students in the school, achieved through positive reinforcement.
- A realistic awareness that evaluation data are only aids to teaching

and learning, and as such are only useful when linked to other information available about students, classes and whole school structure.

- The importance of including multiple perspectives in the school self-evaluation process.
- Being realistic about the capacity of staff for using the data. This includes providing adequate technical support for staff, knowing the boundaries of their capacity in terms of resource and ensuring the data is user friendly and accessible.

CONCLUSIONS

We hope that the research evidence presented in this chapter, as well as reports from practitioners, enhance teachers' knowledge of the value added methodology and also encourage their use of value added feedback and other types of data to evaluate practice. A valid framework for school and teacher self-evaluation needs to incorporate at least four dimensions of effectiveness (in terms of different outcomes, pupil groups, cohorts and curriculum stages) and also needs to contextualise the results with regional or policy information. Moreover, other outcome areas (such as vocational and affective/social) and more direct measures of the quality of teaching and learning need to be incorporated to provide additional feedback that teachers can use to evaluate their success in relation to the broader aims of schooling. Feedback of this kind will inform teachers' learning and evaluation of their own educational practices and capacity for improvement as well as make transparent the constraints, boundaries and context of a school's effectiveness.

NOTES

1 Total GCSE scores have been transformed to normal scores – see Thomas (1999) for further details of analysis.

REFERENCES

DfEE (1998a) *The Autumn Package: pupil performance information*, London: Department for Education and Employment.
DfEE (1998b) *1998 Value Added Pilot: supplement to the secondary school performance tables*, London: Department for Education and Employment.
Elliot, K., Smees, R. and Thomas, S. (1998) 'Making the most of your data:

school self-evaluation using value added measures', *Improving Schools Journal* 1:3, 59–67.

Goldstein, H. (1997) 'Methods in school effectiveness research', *School Effectiveness and School Improvement* 8:4, 369–395.

Gray, J., Goldstein, H. and Jesson, D. (1996) 'Changes and improvements in schools' effectiveness: trends over five years', *Research Papers in Education* 11:1, 35–51.

Gray, J., Hopkins, D., Reynolds, D., Wilcox, B., Farrell, S. and Jesson, D. (1999) *Improving Schools: performance and potential*, Buckingham: Open University Press

Mortimore, P. (1998) *The Road to Improvement: reflections on school effectiveness*, Lisse: Swets and Zeitlinger

Mortimore, P., Sammons, P., Stoll, L., Lewis, D. and Ecob, R. (1988) *School Matters: the junior years*, Wells: Open Books.

Saunders, L. (1998) *'Value Added' Measurement of School Effectiveness: an overview*, Slough: National Foundation for Education Research.

Scheerens, J. and Bosker, R. (1997) *The Foundations of Educational Effectiveness*, Oxford: Elsevier Science.

Smees, R. and Thomas, S. (1998) 'Valuing pupils' views about school', *British Journal of Curriculum and Assessment* 8:3, 8–11.

Thomas, S. (1998) 'Value added measures of school effectiveness in the United Kingdom', *Prospects* 28:1, 91–108.

Thomas, S. (1999) *Optimal Multilevel Models of School Effectiveness: comparative analysis across regions*, ESRC End of Award Report, London: University of London Institute of Education.

Thomas, S. and Mortimore, P. (1996) 'Comparison of value added models for secondary school effectiveness', *Research Papers in Education* 11:1, 5–33.

Thomas, S., Sammons, P., Mortimore, P. and Smees, R. (1997) 'Stability and consistency in secondary schools' effects on students' GCSE outcomes over three years', *School Effectiveness and School Improvement* 8:2, 169–197.

Thomas, S., Smees, R., MacBeath, J., Robertson, P. and Boyd, B. (2000) 'Valuing pupils' views in Scottish schools', *Educational Research and Evaluation* 6:3.

11 Using your initiative – feedback to an LEA on a school improvement initiative

Brenda Taggart and Pam Sammons

INTRODUCTION

This chapter widens the concept of feedback to the part that can be played by outside evaluators in helping a local education authority (LEA) to evaluate its contribution to raising school standards. It is set within the context of a particular school improvement initiative. In 1995 the Belfast Education and Library Board (BELB) in Northern Ireland commissioned members of the International School Effectiveness and Improvement Centre (ISEIC), a centre within the Assessment, Guidance and Effective Learning (AGEL) group of the Institute of Education to externally evaluate a major school improvement initiative. The feedback given to the LEA on this initiative can be seen as a vehicle that assisted organisational learning and helps to demonstrate the extent to which the LEA itself was a learning organisation. As a result of this feedback the LEA was able to look critically at its management of other school improvement initiatives targeted at raising school standards.

It has been claimed that school improvement is an inquiry not a formula and that 'the successful structure for school improvement will have the nature of a clinical science, where communities of educators treat their best ideas as stepping stones to better ones' (Joyce *et al.* 1999: 2). The Making Belfast Work, Raising School Standards (MBW RSS) initiative can be seen as exemplifying such a process. Individual schools involved in the initiative engaged in self-evaluation and review as an integral part of the initiative. The fourteen schools also worked together during the three years on the project sharing experiences and approaches, creating a wider learning community outside the individual school. The LEA's engagement in the process was threefold; manager, participant and an evaluator of the change process. The external evaluation, however, provided the LEA with an objective framework within which to consider organisational learning at a range of levels.

Managing educational change and the resultant organisational learning is

> [a] multivariate business that requires us to think of and address more than one factor at a time. While theory and practice of successful educational change do make sense, and do point to clear guidelines for action, it is always the case that particular actions in particular situations require integrating the more general knowledge of change with detailed knowledge of the politics, personalities and history peculiar to the setting in question.
>
> (Fullan 1991: xii)

In evaluating the MBW RSS initiative it is important to acknowledge the context of civil unrest which for over a generation has been an everyday fact of life for people living in the city. Recent political initiatives to move forward the peace process have been welcomed by all who are concerned about the quality of life in Belfast although uncertainty about the future remains evident.

The term 'feedback', in education, is perhaps most commonly used in classroom and school contexts. It can, however, be used across the education system to promote organisational and institutional learning. In this chapter, we focus on the role of the external evaluation as a method of providing feedback to

- increase understanding of the various impacts of an educational improvement initiative;
- improve awareness of the processes of implementation at school and LEA level; and
- provide the basis for analysis of planning, implementation of future initiatives, enhancing the capacity of the LEA to evaluate its own organisational learning with regard to future initiatives involving clusters or individual schools.

The extent to which an organisation can learn from feedback from an outside evaluation depends on a number of factors. The very act of commissioning shows a willingness to be scrutinised and a desire to learn from an experience. In the MBW RSS there was a climate within both the LEA and schools which suggested that they could effect change and raise standards. Participants were willing to ask difficult questions and challenge practice. A high degree of co-operation among participants and an honest willingness to talk about strengths and weaknesses were important prerequisites for organisational learning. However, many school improvement initiatives have fallen short of their stated objectives because managers have tried to change too much, too quickly. If learning is to take place there must be a tacit understanding that this will not happen for all participants at the same time. Finally there was an acceptance by participants that if this initiative was not going to be just another one of many, which would have little impact beyond set funding, plans and systems had to be put in place which would sustain learning.

LEAs are charged with the duty of managing and monitoring 'school improvement' in their schools. There are many ways in which an LEA might approach this function. Areas for improvement could be identified in Educational Development Plan (EDPs) and targeted through programmes for continual professional development (CDP). Perhaps the most common mechanism used to stimulate school improvement by an LEA is the formulation and management of 'school improvement initiatives'. The recent implementation of national initiatives in England (e.g. the National Literacy and Strategy and Numeracy Hour in primary schools) has not stopped LEAs from continuing to develop locally targeted projects aimed at raising school standards.

So how can an LEA receive feedback on its school improvement initiatives in order to improve its own performance and demonstrate that it is a learning organisation?

Most recently, inspection has been one route by which the performance of school improvement initiatives has been monitored (the programme began in January 1998). The Office of Standards in Education (OFSTED) underlines the important contribution an LEA can make in delivering school improvement by calling its framework for LEA inspection 'LEA support for school improvement', picking out school improvement as an LEA's 'key function' (OFSTED 1999: 6). However, the Chief Inspector of schools in his annual report (1998/1999) claimed that some LEAs gave ineffective support to schools and could spawn 'a plethora of ineffective and often unwelcome initiatives which, more often than not, waste money and confuse and irritate schools' (p. 20). The extent to which OFSTED can give detailed feedback on initiatives, sufficient to ensure organisational learning, is limited because inspections use a national framework and thus do not focus on the aims of different LEA initiatives.

An alternative to inspection would be to use outside consultants to evaluate a specific programme. If an LEA is to make use of an evaluation to improve its services, the evaluator's feedback can identify areas in which the LEA can 'learn' and should indicate how that 'learning' can be transferred to other initiatives.

In evaluating the Making Belfast Work Raising Schools Standards initiative, the ISEIC team were specifically asked to investigate the impact of the overall project and to identify the factors which facilitated improvements and any barriers to success. The BELB, which has a history of innovative projects, wished to consider the implications of the evaluation with a mind to examining other school improvement projects and its part within these.

The idea for the initiative stemmed from thinking in the Department of Education: Northern Ireland (DENI) which approached Making Belfast Work as funders. The initiative intended to help schools address significant disadvantage and under-achievement among their pupils. The project was intended to target a small number of secondary schools and their main contributory primary schools. Additional funding of £3m, over a three-year period was to be allocated.

This chapter cannot report on all aspects of the evaluation covered in the main evaluation report (Sammons *et al.* 1998; Taggart and Sammons 1999) but will focus on ways in which the evaluation's final report was able to feed back key learning points to the LEA, relevant to its management of future school improvement initiatives and the extent to which the initiative had an impact in term of its stated aims. The feedback was couched in terms that were intended to enable BELB's personnel to engage with their own learning and thus better understand their crucial role in initiating and managing initiatives. By doing this, the evaluators sought to help the Board improve its capacity to learn and thus enrich the service it offered to schools in the crucial area of raising school standards. The aspects of the initiative reported here will also be those common to other raising school standards projects in order to identify wider issues of good practice. The specific elements of the initiative addressed here are:

- the launching and selection of schools;
- management;
- action planning;
- financial arrangements;
- support for school;
- the impact on schools;
- factors which contributed to success; and
- factors which were barriers to success.

THE AIM OF THE PROJECT

The project focused on four secondary schools (two maintained Catholic and two controlled Protestant) identified as having high levels of under-achievement and their ten main feeder primary schools. The project aimed to help these schools address significant disadvantage and under-achievement among their pupils and enable them to raise standards, to improve the outcomes of education and academic achievements of pupils, to increase pupil self-confidence and ultimately their employability. At the time low levels of literacy and numeracy were recognised as having a significant impact on later employment prospects and ability to function in adult life (ALBSU 1993).

The primary aim of the project was to provide additional support and resources to schools with the overall objective of accelerating an improvement in the performance and employability of school leavers by improving:

- the quality of management, teaching and learning within the school;
- standards of literacy and numeracy;
- the level of qualifications;
- links with local industry;
- parental involvement;
- discipline in class; and
- attendance and punctuality.

The areas for improvement targeted by this initiative mirror those identified by Barber and Dann (1996) who produced a very similar list to the one above when analysing questionnaire responses from schools involved in sixty UK urban initiatives designed to produce 'higher pupil attainment' (p. 69).

THE EVALUATION

The evaluation adopted a case study approach recognising both the overall aims of the initiative *and* the differing aims of individual schools.

Unlike OFSTED inspections, the evaluation did not focus only on pupil outcomes, although these were held to be crucial indicators of success. The use of interviews and questionnaires from teachers and pupils ensured that these important 'players in the piece' were given the opportunity for their 'voices' to be heard. One of the limitations of addressing the impact on outcomes was the absence of common base-line measures of prior attainment across all participating schools. This prevented the analysis of pupil progress in all but a minority of schools.

Launching the initiative and selection of schools

A number of difficulties were encountered at the start of the project in relation to the launch of the initiative and selection of schools. Some confusion existed as to the selection criteria used, although the evaluation indicated that the stated criteria were applied correctly. Greater attention to planning prior to the official start of work with schools, could have alleviated some of these teething problems.

It should be remembered that any project involving the distribution of significant extra resources is bound to create tensions between apparent 'winners' and 'losers'. Moreover, the identification of under-achieving schools, and the attendant publicity, likewise create considerable pressures on schools and have an impact on morale. Against this must be set the positive impact of the provision of support and resources to assist schools in the improvement process. The feed-back given to the LEA sought to enable senior managers to grapple with the difficult decisions which have to be faced when schools are singled out for inclusion in development projects. LEAs have be been seen to be supporting schools which are experiencing difficulties with-out appearing to reward under-performance.

Management

The complexities of managing a major three-year initiative were examined. The work of co-ordinators in schools and the need for Senior Management Teams (SMT) support, especially from the Principal was highlighted. The work of Advisers (LEA personnel) and Field Officers (advisory teachers seconded to the LEA) was positively regarded, though time and workload pressures inevitably limited their input in individual schools.

A Central Management Committee (CMC) was convened to ensure that the initiative was effectively managed. It had a key role in moni-toring, allocating finances, setting timetables and making policy decisions. When managing an initiative by committee there is always a balance to be struck between strategic and administrative duties. There was the perception by some that, in the first year, the CMC's agenda was overtaken by administration (given the large sums of money to be allocated) and it became a 'budget debating group'. In December 1994, the CMC divided into a 'steering' group' and a 'management' group. The former was responsible for the allocation of resources and the latter played the major role in school development issues, e.g. the development of 'exit' strategies to plan for the end of the project. It is notable that participating schools had no representation on the CMC.

In schools the management of the initiative was overseen by the Governing Body and the Principal. The day-to-day management was the responsibility of a designated RSS co-ordinator who was usually an experienced senior member of staff. An unclear role and insufficient involvement of schools' governing bodies appeared to have been a general difficulty and greater involvement of these in monitoring and evaluating their schools' RSS activities might have proved helpful.

The perspective of the funders (MBW) was also reported. In the early stages of the initiative, the specific management responsibilities were not made entirely clear. This caused some difficulties for the funders who became unsure of the structure for accountability. During the final year of the initiative MBW had a representative on the CMC, they also attended some meetings between BELB advisers and school personnel. This more direct involvement with BELB and school personnel, through the regular update meetings, helped to reassure MBW, as funders, that the initiative was being effectively and efficiently managed. It is important that any funders of initiatives consider having representation on relevant management bodies and that they ensure that all initiatives are properly audited/evaluated so that strengths can be built on and any weaknesses addressed.

The operational side of the initiative was largely in the hands of BELB officers and advisers. The advisers and field officers saw themselves as the interface between schools and the management arm of the initiative (CMC). Advisers felt they needed more time *before* the start of the initiative to share expertise, experience from other projects, to formulate strategies for consistency in dealing with schools, to set up operational procedures and, perhaps most importantly, to familiarise themselves with the key elements of initiating, developing and sustaining school improvement.

All advisers had a considerable workload associated with their subject or age phase specialisms. At the time of RSS they were also involved with the introduction of Staff Development Performance Reviews and a review of the Northern Ireland National Curriculum and assessment arrangements. The additional work generated by the

RSS placed a 'heavy burden' on already full diaries. This inevitably affected the amount of time officers and advisers were able to give to RSS schools and the amount of contact they had with some schools was often reported to be 'managed on workloads as opposed to the needs of the school'.

Action planning

School development planning is an important tool in school improvement initiatives (MacGilchrist *et al.* 1995). At the beginning of the project, schools were asked to submit an Action Plan identifying how they would operationalise the RSS initiative. Schools and advisers were generally unfamiliar with the demands of action planning and target setting at the start of the project. None the less this was an area in which great gains were made during the course of the three-year project. An enhanced capacity to plan and manage change and to monitor and evaluate developments and their outcomes was a very positive achievement in most schools. Participants reported a much greater awareness of school effectiveness and improvement issues and believed that the bringing together of schools and resources to undertake significant staff development work had broadened their perspectives.

Enhanced schools' capacities to plan and develop collaborative ways of planning and working should continue to reap substantial benefits to schools in the longer term after the cessation of an initiative.

Financial arrangements

The MBW RSS initiative involved the allocation of considerable additional resources to schools and this inevitably placed a burden on the BELB and on individual schools to ensure that moneys were properly accounted for. The project was set up to address identified needs, and schools were required to conduct an analysis of needs before bidding in their Action Plans for additional funds. Difficulties related to a mismatch between the constraints of the financial year (with spending plans needing to be agreed by end of March) and those of the school year caused problems, particularly in the first year.

There were complaints about hurried decisions and distraction by budgetary matters from the attention the co-ordinators and SMT in schools could spend engaging in improvement work. None the less, all respondents were extremely positive about MBW's commitment to provide substantial additional funds.

Not all schools received funding for all aspects of their Action Plans. The evidence suggests that, in the first year, some schools' Action Plans were over-ambitious, and that they needed to be encouraged to focus on specific and manageable goals. There were some concerns in certain schools about the management of the process of deciding which aspects of Action Plans bids would be funded. Greater transparency about how decisions are reached can go a long way to relieving anxieties about finding.

There were some dangers that the MBW RSS could become a funding-led initiative, and the BELB and MBW were keen that this school improvement initiative would be sustained beyond the official end of funding. Considerable effort was put into helping schools plan their exit strategies during the third year of the study to help sustain the impact of the work.

Support for schools

In addition to direct financial support, the BELB allocated advisers and later field officers with curriculum expertise to work with the project schools. In the first year these advisers felt they were not well prepared for the challenging task they were set and would have liked specific training e.g. in action planning and evaluation methods *prior* to the project's inception. None the less they felt they learnt a great deal on the job as the initiative progressed and commented on the value of the wider perspective on school effectiveness/improvement which they developed as a result of various development activities.

Both advisers and field officers were perceived by schools to have provided very valuable additional support, particularly in relation to action planning and staff development. This was seen to have led to real curriculum development and improvement in the quality of teaching and learning, particularly in relation to literacy, and to a lesser extent mathematics in most schools. Inevitably, pressures of time and workload limited the amount of support given by advisers and field officers, although in some schools it was felt to be 'hard' to get past the SMT to work with teachers and thus officers could not provide all the support they felt was needed.

Advisers felt they had played a particularly important role in helping schools identify needs and in the action planning process, although with hindsight they felt they had become too involved with budgets and the financial cycle which distracted their energies from the more important task of curriculum development.

The impact of the MBW RSS on schools

Evidence was presented in the evaluation feedback in relation to the extent of improvement as perceived by different groups of stakeholders (teachers, pupils, parents) surveyed in all schools. The perceptions and views of key personnel (Principals and Co-ordinators in schools, Chairs of Governors, advisers and field officers) involved in implementing, overseeing or managing the initiative as a whole were also explored. These provided qualitative evidence concerning perceptions of improvement and the contribution of RSS in effecting positive change in the various foci of the RSS initiative.

Statistical data (examination results, reading or mathematics scores, attendance and suspensions) were also reported where available. These provide quantitative evidence about the impact on standards.

The areas covered include:

- teaching and learning;
- educational standards;
- local industry;
- parental involvement;
- discipline and behaviour;
- primary–secondary links; and
- pupil motivation and satisfaction.

There was general agreement that the MBW RSS experience had been very beneficial in promoting curriculum and staff development in schools and that this had led to improvements in the quality of teaching and learning in most schools. Better resources, staff collaboration and more time for planning were seen as particularly positive outcomes.

Overall, the evaluation indicated that all schools were now placing a much greater emphasis on measuring and monitoring pupil outcomes, particularly in the basic skills. Several schools had introduced baseline screening for all year groups and were using this to monitor subsequent progress and to help plan their special needs provision. Unfortunately, because not all schools instituted baseline screening at the start of the project and due to variations in the year group focus, it was not possible to make systematic comparisons of pupil progress across either the four secondary or the ten primaries involved. An expanded RSSI which commenced a year later in 1995, by contrast, adopted a rigorous approach to base-lining specific year groups using common measures thus enabling value added analyses of pupil progress to be conducted in future years (Thomas and Sammons 1996).

The evaluation evidence suggests that reading standards had been raised in several of the MBW RSS schools, through the introduction of specific structured school-wide or targeted reading programmes. The considerable challenges faced by schools, particularly the four secondaries, in terms of low levels of skills of entrants must be acknowledged. The highly selective nature of the Belfast education system (which still retains the eleven-plus) and the high levels of socioeconomic disadvantage are reflected in the intakes of the RSS schools and this context should be remembered.

The results of our evaluation's analysis of pupil progress where data were available suggest that these specific structured school-wide programmes led to short-term reading gains in several schools. If these gains are sustained they should have a positive impact on subsequent progress and eventually on later public examination results. The evaluation indicated that some schools were seeking to extend their success in reading to promoting numeracy. As yet, however, there was little to suggest the same kind of structured, whole school approach was being developed. The Numeracy Task Force (DfEE 1998), suggests that structured approaches to mathematics teaching may be especially beneficial for promoting basic numeracy skills, and that this may be particularly valuable for schools serving disadvantaged communities. Schools serving such communities may benefit from guidance on such approaches to further extend their approaches to numeracy.

Poor pupil behaviour, attendance and discipline were a source of grave concern in several schools prior to the initiative. Teachers reported general improvements in schools' approaches to these matters, although change in the incidence of poor behaviour was felt to be modest.

Factors which contributed to success

A variety of factors were identified as contributing to the successful implementation of the MBW RSS project.

The provision of significant extra resources provided important new opportunities for schools to engage in curriculum and staff development. Smaller classes, more time for planning and new materials and equipment were all noted.

The MBW RSS project provided a valuable forum for discussion and sharing of good practice and encouraged a greater focus on teaching and learning and classroom management issues. Schools reported greater collegiality in approaches and a greater sense of whole school vision as a result of being part of the initiative.

The schools received extra support from BELB advisers and field officers which was seen to have facilitated improvement. Schools' staff were also encouraged to take responsibility for developing their own improvement strategies and developed their capacity for action planning, monitoring and evaluation.

Principal support was seen to be crucial to the success of the MBW RSS project in schools. By contrast, in schools where there were significant weaknesses in the existing SMT, implementing the project proved difficult. Hallinger's (1996) review of the role of the Principal in school effectiveness research provides evidence of this link.

Factors which were barriers to success

The relatively short time scale of the three-year project was regarded as insufficient for improvement to be adequately demonstrated in schools by all involved in the initiative. A five-year time scale may be more realistic in studying school change.

Problems in the mismatch of the demands of the financial and school years were felt to have made action planning problematic, especially in the first year.

Long-standing difficulties relating to poor management, in some schools, were not always seen to have been adequately dealt with. This limited the work of co-ordinators and advisers. Amalgamation (past and present) was seen to have caused particular difficulties in certain schools.

During the launch the public naming of the four secondaries in particular was felt to have adversely affected staff morale and attitudes to the MBW RSS in the first year.

Lack of prior training for advisers meant that much learning was done on the job and they felt they initially lacked the necessary expertise to advise on the action planning process, and on base-lining and evaluation strategies. The availability of DENI Inspection Reports in several school at the start of the project was felt to have aided the process of 'needs analysis' and action planning.

The workload implications of a school improvement initiative must be recognised and additional staff need to be assigned early in the project, so that workloads can be managed in a way that reduces stress on individuals.

The absence of an audit of previous curriculum and improvement projects in the Education and Library Boards also meant that the MBW RSS was not always able to build on the strengths of previous initiatives.

CONCLUSIONS

Much was learnt from the MBW RSS experience, both by individual schools and by BELB personnel. As with any initiative, there were areas of success and aspects where less progress was made than anticipated. Schools significantly developed their capacity to plan, monitor and evaluate school improvement, and the quality of teaching and learning was improved in many cases. None the less, significant challenges remained in several schools, especially at the secondary level. Some positive effects on pupils' reading were identified, and attempts to transfer this success to mathematics were being made. Behaviour, discipline and attendance remained areas of concern, although modest improvements in attendance were found in most schools.

On the whole, secondary schools faced greater challenges and experienced more difficulties in implementing their improvement strategies than their feeder primaries. The extent to which schools can overcome the impact of disadvantage is open to debate (see discussion by Mortimore and Whitty 1997).

As yet the long-term benefits of the MBW RSS initiative are hard to judge, given the three-year time scale. There is evidence that the experience of the project's first year provided a helpful input into the planning process for the expanded RSSI province-wide which involved all five Education and Library Boards in Northern Ireland.

The MBW RSS initiative provides an important example of a school improvement initiative which had very clear and laudable aims focusing on promoting pupil outcomes and which combined considerable financial support with external advice and guidance in seeking to develop participating schools' capacity to improve. It thus attempted to integrate both a 'top down', external approach to improvement with the encouragement of 'bottom up' strategies developed within individual schools. The majority of those involved valued the opportunity this provided and believed that much had been learnt as a result.

The evaluators were able to feed back to the BELB not only on specifics within the initiative. Two other very important sections included in the evaluation report were:

- the legacy of RSS and challenges for the future; and
- implications of RSS experience for other school improvement initiatives.

The evaluation report alone was insufficient to provide the level of feedback which really enriched the learning process. After the report was delivered a conference was held with the evaluators and representatives of all those involved in the initiative. This was essential in the feedback process as it:

- enabled participants to explore various sections of the report with the authors;
- provided a forum for discussion within and across groups of stakeholders;
- enabled participants to reflect on the learning that had taken place both at an individual and group level; and
- initiated discussion on future developments.

The evaluation team, as a direct result of giving this more intimate verbal feedback, subsequently returned to Belfast to work with key LEA personnel on developmental work in the field of school improvement and school effectiveness.

The 'evaluation' of the 'evaluation' emphasised the importance of feedback, both written and verbal. The LEA was better able to consider its capacity to act as a learning organisation, make connections across its function and help schools in the difficult task of raising their standards. External evaluation has an important part to play in providing feedback to organisations to help them make a significant difference to the lives of children.

REFERENCES

ALBSU (1993) *The Basic Skills of Young Adults*, London: ALSBU.

Barber, M. and Dann, R. (eds) (1996) *Raising Educational Standards in the Inner City: practical initiatives in action*, London: Cassell.

DfEE (1998) *Numeracy Matters: The preliminary report of the Numeracy Task Force*, London: DfEE.

Fullan, M. (1991) *The New Meaning of Educational Change*, London: Cassell.

Hallinger, P. (1996) 'The Principal's role in school effectiveness: an assessment of substantive findings 1980–1995', paper presented at the Annual Meeting of the American Educational Research Association, New York.

Joyce, B., Calhoun, E. and Hopkins, D. (1999) *The New Structure of School Improvement: inquiring schools and achieving students*, Buckingham: Open University Press.

MacGilchrist, B., Mortimore, P., Savage, J. and Beresford, C. (1995) *Planning Matters: the impact of development planning in primary schools*, London: Paul Chapman.

Mortimore, P. and Whitty, G. (1997) *Can School Improvement Overcome the*

Effects of Disadvantage?, London: University of London Institute of Education.

OFSTED (1998/99) *The Annual Report of Her Majesty's Chief Inspector of Schools: standards and quality in education*, London: Stationery Office.

OFSTED (1999) *LEA Support for School Improvement*, London: Stationery Office.

Sammons, P., Taggart, B. and Thomas, S. (1998) *Making Belfast Work: Raising School Standards – An Evaluation: report prepared for the Belfast Education and Library Board*, London: ISEIC University of London Institute of Education.

Taggart. B. and Sammons. P. (1999) 'Evaluating the impact of a raising school standards initiative', in R. J. Bosker, B. P. M. Creemers and S. Stringfield (eds) *Enhancing Educational Excellence, Equity and Efficiency: evidence from evaluations of systems and schools in change*, Dordrecht: Kluwer.

Thomas, S. and Sammons, P. (1996) *Raising School Standards Initiative: the development of baseline and value added measures for DENI*, London: ISEIC University of London Institute of Education.

Index